# SHADOW
# COMPANION

A Life Journey Navigating
The Mire of Racism.

## HYMERS WILSON

ISBN 978-1-990543-27-2 (Softcover)
ISBN 978-1-990543-22-7 (Hardcover)

All photos from family sources.

The information and stories contained in this book are presented to the best of the author's recollection and are told from his perspective. The author has made every effort to portray events, places, and people as faithfully and accurately as possible, however some errors, omissions, or inaccuracies may exist. The author takes no responsibility for any such errors, omissions, or inaccuracies.

Edited by Daphne Ffoulkes-Jones. Copyedited by Leah Green
Cover and interior design by Ashley Russell Designs
Published by NextGen Story: Custom Publishing
www.nextgenstory.com

# Contents

# ACKNOWLEDGEMENTS

I'd like to thank Hymers Wilson Sr. (deceased) for his example of how to be a husband, a father, and a man.

To my mother, Dahlia Wilson, thank you for your quiet strength and example of resilience.

Thank you, Joy, my wife and companion, for your kindness and love, evident ever since the day you ironed my Master of Divinity graduation gown more than four decades ago.

To my dear children, Hermione, Hannah, and Hymers III, you are a testament to the fact that our parenting worked. I thank you for your interest in my story, which in many ways is our story. I bequeath it to you to pass on to the next generation.

Thank you, Pastor Halsey Peat, for being my confidant with whom I could also discuss the ideas for my book. I thank both you and your wife, Marisol Fermin-Peat, and your children, Dina and Annia Peat, for being constant friends of our family for the past four decades.

I thank you sincerely, Keith Lockhart, for your enduring friendship, advice, and input into this project.

I am grateful to you, my friend, Dr. Jeffrey Brown, for planting the seed of the idea that writing a book is a possibility.

Thank you to my Publishing Managers, Mali Bain and Shayna Lewis; my Structural Editor, Daphne Ffoulks-Jones; my Copyeditor, Leah Green; and my Designer, Ashley Russell of NextGen Story: Custom Publishing, for your invaluable assistance in making the dream of this book a reality.

I thank God who has guided my ancestors through rising and setting suns and the shadows in-between.

# FOREWORD
## Keith Lockhart

When I was a young Seventh-day Adventist in East London, my family made a yearly trip into town to Westminster Central Hall. It is a grand Methodist building and we would go there for a day of fellowship, which attracted myriads of Adventists across the capital.

I first saw Hymers at one of these gatherings. He was onstage in my memory, saying something about youth work at his home church in Holloway in North London. A smart young man around age twenty, he spoke well in a rich and clear voice. He was five years older than me, too distant at that time for me to get near enough to speak to him.

But I already knew a little of his family. His father was well known in London Adventist circles after appearing in a television documentary on Adventism, which I watched when our pastor showed it in one of our church meetings. His father was also on the local lay preacher circuit and he came to our church one day. I can still remember the sermon: he preached against the Beatles after one of them scandalized much of the Christian world by claiming the band was more popular than Jesus. I was a fan of the group and his father's unsettling words rang in my ears for weeks.

The family had thus made quite the impression on me before I talked to Hymers for the first time, shortly after I started at the Adventist-run Newbold College in England. It was the autumn of 1977 on a campus set, as Hymers well describes in this book, in the rolling Berkshire countryside–a world away from where I was from in London.

Hymers spotted me in the cafeteria while I was in the queue working out what I was going to get for lunch. He asked where I was from and I said London. He also asked, probably sensing I was feeling a little homesick, whether I had any plans to go home for a weekend during the term. I said I didn't, as I was skint (a word we used in London for having no money). "Skint," he smiled. "I haven't heard that word for a while." Our shared understanding of one cockney word formed an instant bond between us.

At Newbold, I quickly grew to admire his ready wit and even temperament. I witnessed, too, his various gifts as public speaker, editor, five-a-side footballer, and, above all, his talent for friendship. As far as I could tell, his only failing was his devotion to North London's Arsenal Football Club. Living further east, my local team was West Ham. But as he teased me when my support for the Hammers came out, "We can't all be perfect."

Our London backgrounds were not the only thing we shared as we both were the sons of West Indian parents who had immigrated to England in the 1950s. We also both did well enough in primary school to pass the Eleven Plus exam, a rite of passage to a better education in the state sector. For kids like us, that meant advancing to classrooms where there were only one or two other kids like us.

A particular delight to me is Hymers' recounting of what this was like. On the one hand, you had great fun with your mates who accepted you–especially if you were clever and played football (football was the great equaliser in the playground, the place where racial differences disappeared). On the other, the racism that came from being in an over-whelmingly White environment was something from which you could never entirely escape.

As you turn these pages, you won't be able to avoid it either for racism is this memoir's inescapable theme. Like Banquo's ghost, it is the spectre at the feast, the guest in the house who never leaves. Hymers calls it a "shadow companion," a travel partner who accompanied him wherever he went in life. You'll find out here how it followed him to school, sat next to him in the pews at church, turned up in college and at work, and boarded the plane with him when he migrated himself to North America. Hymers brings out the full personality of this malevolent partner–how it talks, what it does, the way it moves, and the ill-consid-ered manner with which it intrudes on relationships.

Anyone who knows Hymers will be well aware that he wouldn't tell this tale without leavening it with his customary good humour. As he sent me extracts of what he was writing, I would burst out laughing at an anecdote, a mocking schoolboy song, or a particularly hilarious encounter with some local boys when he was on a visit to the land of his parents.

Hymers' story adds to a growing body of literature in which the children of the Black immigrants who came to England after the Second World War collate their experiences. They don't all tell the same story as each one was determined to a large degree by the corner of England where the author grew up. For example, Afua Hirsch's *Brit(ish)* evolved from a privately educated girlhood in Wimbledon while Clive Myrie's *Everything is Everything* was moulded by his upbringing in Bolton, Lancashire.

Hymers' *Shadow Companion* was shaped by North London. It's a story of hope and achievement, pain and disappointment. By reading it, I'm confident that whatever your own background–Black, White or Brown–you'll be all the richer for it.

# PREFACE

I used to think that only nationally known politicians, journalists, actors, and sports personalities had lives interesting enough to write autobiographies. More recently, I began to believe that the biographies of ordinary people like me are indeed worthy of attention–at least from the immediate family members who will come after them. There are also contemporaries who, in this increasingly small world, briefly intersected with my life before travelling on to other places, who never knew about my journey in its complex fullness. There is the wider public, too, who I believe can learn lessons of resilience from my albeit humble path, which never made the front page of any form of media (social or otherwise).

So, I offer my story about my unique struggles and perspective on life as I navigated bright days as well as times overcast with dark shadows. I am part of a diaspora of West Indians who moved from the Caribbean to industrial giants such as the United Kingdom, the United States, and Canada, seeking employment, education, and a legacy of financial stability for generations to come. For this reason, I didn't grow up surrounded by a large, extended family, which is instead scattered around the world. It is thus imperative for me that my story becomes a record for any of them who might explore the path our part of the family took.

Writing this book was a task that took me four years, providing a learning exercise in patience and humility. I had written term papers for my post-secondary degrees and articles for church magazines before, but this in comparison was a marathon that took four years to complete. The COVID-19 pandemic, which began in 2020 as I was returning from a trip to Ghana, gave me the opportunity, time, and space to reflect more fully on my life and I wrote down some of the details of my journey while cloistered in enforced isolation in my home in Oshawa, Ontario. Once restrictions eased, I was able to resume my winter getaways and write some more in the warmth of the Caribbean in Barbados.

I am grateful to my dear friend Keith Lockhart, who is also an author, for reviewing the book and providing both feedback and affirmation. I am especially thankful for the guidance of my publishing manager, Mali Bain. While in Barbados, I wondered how to get my book "out the door" (a phrase I used often with Mali). I came across a workshop for people interested in writing their life stories that she was conducting via Zoom from British Columbia for the Oshawa Senior Community Centre in Ontario. From that meeting, she kindly agreed to help me through the process of polishing and producing my book.

We live in a world where division and distrust are part and parcel of the landscape. I wrote my book to reveal how I have experienced it and met its challenges. At times, I write analytically of such situations. Other times, I write from my heart. While this latter writing may be jarring to the reader, I want to make it clear that I do not intend to create further division with my words. I simply want the authenticity of my voice to come through in the expression of my feelings, following the biblical principle that " ... the truth will set you free" (John 8:32 CEV). Truth promotes reconciliation.

I dedicate this book to my wife and constant companion for the past forty-two years, Joy Anne, and to my children Hermione Dale, Hannah Rachel, and Hymers Augustus III.

Daughter Hermione

Daughter Hannah

Son Hymers III

My Joy and constant companion for over 40 years.

# INTRODUCTION

I have lived a full life that unfolded in England, the United States, and Canada. With each passing year, my fortunes were much like a roller coaster ride–sometimes up and sometimes down. But through it all, I survived with my intact self-esteem bolstered by my roots and the guidance of my Jamaican parents. They had migrated to England from Jamaica, seeking a better educational and financial future for themselves. Even more importantly, they wanted this future for their children whose good fortunes they felt would have been less attainable in the West Indies.

My book follows my journey from Jamaica to my early childhood in post-war North London, England, through my primary, secondary, and post-secondary education as I sought to establish myself and achieve financial independence. I was all too aware that as a child of immigrants, failure to do well in school meant an infinitely harder road ahead. This meant navigating a world that appeared benign on the surface, but had a dark and menacing interloper. Most times, you wouldn't see it or hear it or even be remotely aware of it. Other times, it was in your face. Still, its shadowy presence dogged my journey across the seas to the United States where I spent a total of two years, first at university in Michigan and later training to be a chaplain at a medical centre in Ohio. It was the menace of racism, whose shadow accompanied me even when I eventually settled in Canada where I currently reside.

Without the preparation I received from my parents to chart my course through life, I might not have survived so well. They instilled in me a belief and unwavering trust in God to get one through any obstacles that emerged. They were well aware of racism–but God was more powerful, their humour more uplifting, and their creativity, work ethic, and energy more than a match for the dark forces they encountered. They knew that education was another key ingredient for survival and expanding one's horizons through literature was vital to the resilience that kept me safe. I took on their approach to life. It kept them stable, and it would become my anchor as well.

You will witness how religion did not always live up to my expectations. The Seventh-day Adventist Church to which I belonged presented itself as home to more faithful followers of God than other religions but the shadow of racism was there, too, as I witnessed its political machinations.

As you read, you'll see my career evolve from that of a pastor to a social worker fulfilling the functions of a crisis support worker, mental health therapist, and counsellor. These occupations were part of my core. I was always most comfortable in the helping professions, a natural outgrowth of my upbringing in a household that took seriously the Christian ethic of being the salt of the earth and blessing one's community by one's presence in it. These values endured despite the disappointment of seeing a church in turmoil over the issue of race.

Getting married and having a family meant passing on the lessons of resilience I received growing up, which were shared by my life partner. When our children were younger, we sometimes shielded them. But as they aged into adolescence and young adulthood, we talked about racism in both its personal and systemic forms so they would be prepared to meet it in what can sometimes be a hostile world for Black youngsters.

I look forward to you joining me as I map out my life's journey and perhaps you'll find encouragement in what kept me safe, sane, and stable through it all. Indeed, my hope is that you'll find lessons of resilience that you too can adopt for yourself in your own journey.

# SHADOW COMPANION
## A Travel Partner

As I write, discussion of Black lives and the vigorous response to the Black Lives Matter protests are unfolding in Washington against a backdrop of restraint shown by police to White rioters who briefly took over the Capitol building there on January 6, 2021. This is where my story begins: every part of my life has been touched by racism. I have always known it, but watching these events unfold has caused this blight to weigh upon my mind like a nagging migraine that just won't go away.

As I journeyed through life, I never dwelled on the racism or subtly dismissive comments I experienced. On a Zoom call with some old friends recently, we all agreed that none of us dwelled on the racism we had encountered. I said (and I think we all agreed) that if we did, it would have driven us crazy. I couldn't have existed or been happy, let alone productive and thriving, if I had constantly lived in that space–nor did I burden my children with the racism my wife and I had felt. Most times, it was as shadowy as Scotch mist. When it was blatant, we pressed on, resisting its clammy embrace with thoughts of survival and an "in spite of" march forward.

It wasn't that we failed to prepare our children for what lay out there in society. Once they were old enough, we talked about racial injustice. We interpreted what we saw in the news and armed them, as best we could, for their own struggles with society and its systems. But as I look back, I can see that I didn't tell them the whole story about my own encounters with systemic racism. So, this book is for my children, in-laws, and others who come after me, whether friend or foe. Its main messages are centred on the resilience and strength I mined to navigate my path in life, and the shadow of racism that followed me.

As an ordained minister of religion, I want to say that the message of this book is also a testament to the human spirit, for our ability to survive and thrive despite the odds against us. As such, anybody–Black, White, Brown, or however one has been categorized–who reads about my experiences can learn lessons of survival as well.

I remember hearing Pastor Charles Bradford, a prominent former leader at the headquarters of my church, preaching a sermon about the exodus of the Israelites from the slavery they encountered in Egypt. He contrasted and compared Egyptian slavery with the experience of Africans enslaved in North America, pointing out the similarities of the experience. Then he made what for me was a novel but welcome leap to the assertion that everybody, Black and White, can learn vital lessons from the experience of slavery.

I already knew instinctively that the ability of Black people to have lived, survived, and even thrived despite the adversity of prejudice and racism was a testament to our indomitable spirit. We had something special that we could pass on to succeeding generations. We had an ability to not just make do, but rise above and prosper no matter what was thrown our way. Here was Charles Bradford explaining that White people also could learn *from us Black people* about resilience in the face of difficulties, which we all actually encounter.

Since then, I have come to an awareness that a destructive perspective has become entrenched through centuries of indoctrination that dehumanizes Black people. White people, particularly those in Europe, the United States, Scandinavia, the Nordic countries, and Europeans beyond, have been scarred by socialization that causes them to avoid and deny the truth of the well-documented history of the plunder, rape, and pillage of Africa and other regions. I am thus aware that even putting this into words may be perceived as an attack by some when in fact that is not my intention. Failure to confront historical excesses has led to a psychological fragility, by which I mean an intolerance for hearing about the terrible history of colonization.

Who, on an individual level, likes being confronted by their mistakes? I am in no way implying that Black people don't make mistakes. Yet as a trained counsellor, I am aware that good mental health involves confronting one's mistakes and learning from them. The psychological fragility I speak of has also led to a fear of Black and Brown people and their capabilities. The dehumanizing indoctrination has led many White people to think of Black people as inherently and unpredictably dangerous.

As a child, I learned how to protect myself from the imposed mental burden of being a visible minority while listening to stories my father told. He would talk about the way he and his Royal Air Force friends from the Caribbean refused to take the prejudice they encountered in World War II England without a fight. I learned from my dad that speaking up and defending yourself was a way of life: you took no nonsense from anyone. You might be Black and you might not have much, but you had the right to be respected whatever the cost. I didn't always bravely put that learning into practice, choosing out of fear to sometimes keep quiet and not draw negative attention. Still, the stories formed deep within me a foundation of self-esteem that anchored me especially in my adult years.

One day when I was no more than about six years old, my dad, mum, my sister Paula, and I were about to board a red London Transport double decker bus. In those days, the buses had a platform at the back left-hand side. The conductor would stand there, with a small machine that issued tickets strapped to him, to see who was getting on the bus. The conductor looked at me and said cheerily, "Hello, sunshine." Quick as a flash, my father retorted, "His name is Hymers, not sunshine." Whatever the intent of the conductor, my father interpreted his cheery welcome as less than respectful. I had a name, and it wasn't the name the conductor had summarily conferred upon me. In my dad's eyes, there was no way I was going to be diminished.

So here I am, looking back and realizing from the perspective of six decades that racism has been a constant and unwanted shadow companion in my life. This travel partner has been by my side sometimes without me even knowing it was there. My journey would sometimes take a twist and a turn, and I'd only later realize in a moment of clarity that

Photo of my dad flanked by two Royal Air Force buddies during World War II.

this ghostly intruder had sent me on the turns I'd taken. Other times, it was the all-too-present passenger who grabbed me and was in my face, forcing me to recognize its ominous presence.

Looking back has involved carefully examining my life and realizing that racism has had an inescapable impact. Second guessing the intentions of White teachers, supervisors, managers, and occasionally even friends has become a necessary part of my internal processing. My cousin and psychologist, Dr. Jerome Crichton, would say that my experiences have contributed to hypervigilance fostered by mistrust and an almost pathological drive to stay on the right side of the dominant culture. Yet I have also come to the realization that the self-esteem instilled from an early age by my parents and my community formed a bedrock that later helped me survive and even thrive as an individual.

# A FIRM FOUNDATION
## Jamaican Roots

Mum told me that when she first met dad in the parish of Hanover in Jamaica, she was wary of this young man who had come back from serving in the military in England. She was, and still is, a devout Christian with very strict Seventh-day Adventist standards. These included no smoking, no dancing, no card playing, and a list of other things her religion didn't allow. Looking at it positively, her church promoted a healthy lifestyle. Dressing modestly with no rings except a wedding ring for women, no earrings or necklaces, was an indicator of a good Seventh-day Adventist preparing for the Second Coming of Christ. Saturday Sabbath observance meant that every Saturday, mum would have been in church. Vegetarianism among Seventh-day Adventists was promoted back then, in the 1950s, way before it became fashionable. Mum also told me she was determined to not go the way of so many of the other girls in the district, taken advantage of by men who got them pregnant and often didn't hang around to parent their offspring.

So when dad came along as a mere recent convert to her religion, she was wary of him. He seemed like a bit of a ruffian. He asked to walk her home from the church they both attended and at first, she declined. He persisted, saying it was a free country and he could walk where he wanted–and walk with her he would.

He eventually proposed and, worn down by dad's entreaties, mum accepted. A minister was found who would marry them in his own home. At the time, mum was fending for herself as a dressmaker; her own mother had already passed away. At nineteen, she packed her bag and went to the minister's home to wait for my dad for the wedding. When she got there, the minister still hadn't returned from a trip out of town. The minister's wife took mum in and told her the situation. Mum was annoyed that neither the minister nor my dad were there yet and wanted to take off and walk back to where she lived. She says that upon seeing her mood and annoyance, the minister's wife locked mum in her room and wouldn't let her out until eventually the minister and my dad arrived and the wedding took place.

On February 1, 1953, four months before the coronation of Queen Elizabeth II, I was born at my dad's family homestead up in the hills a few miles from Montego Bay. Mum had gone to live there in what had become her new home after the wedding. I am told that the homestead is called Wellington. My birth was registered in Ramble, Hanover.

## ARRIVAL IN ENGLAND

I was brought from Jamaica to England by my mother in 1954 on the SS Auriga, an Italian passenger ship. The urge to move to England was a matter of survival as employment in Jamaica was precarious. At the end of the war, my father was demobilized from the Royal Air Force;

as England changed from a country at war to a country in a state of peace, the military had to be scaled down. Dad was released from active service and had to return to Jamaica from England where he had been based. He found work in the tourism industry serving tables in a hotel. However, he wanted more: an education or a trade for himself and my mother–or at least for the children who would come along later. Opportunities for these things were not so attainable in post-war Jamaica.

My mother told me on the SS Auriga, she succumbed to motion sickness from the heavy seas and I wandered all over the ship on my own. Once the sea sickness passed and she felt able to leave the confines of her cabin, people she didn't know would come up to her and tell her how delightful her little boy was. I was just one and a half years old. When my mother and I arrived in England, we joined my father who had gone ahead of us from the West Indies to find a job and a home to live in. Before he died in 2010, dad told me that he had a place lined up and everything was going according to plan but days before we arrived, that place fell through. He had to scramble around and found another rental literally a day or two before we got there.

I started my life in England at 14 Yonge Park in North London near Finsbury Park. It was a place our family rented from a White couple who either needed the money and was willing to put up with the scorn of their neighbours or just had genuine good hearts at a time when Black people looking for places to rent would be confronted by signs on the doors of houses stating, "No Blacks, no dogs, no Irish." The renter's wife was Mrs. Giraud, who my mother repeatedly lauded as a very kind and fair woman. Not much was ever said to me about her husband, but these were the kind people who presumably were open-minded enough to resist the temptation and pressure to let prejudice guide their decisions. They opened their home to the young Black couple, my mom and dad, and me, the little toddler.

Those were days when milk was delivered to your door by a milkman whose wagon was pulled by a horse. Behind the animal, a burlap bag was hitched. Its droppings were scooped off the road and dumped into the bag–great fertilizer, no doubt, for growing vegetables and other produce.

After some time at Yonge Park, my dad, my mum, me, and my sister Paula (born in August 1955) moved to 24 Dunford Road near the Holloway Road tube station. By today's standards, the living arrangement was challenging. My parents were renting two rooms on the second floor. The stove was on the landing! I'm guessing that anybody going up to the third floor, where another tenant lived, would be privy to the delectable fragrance of my mother's Caribbean cuisine. The Greek Cypriot landlord lived downstairs on the first floor with his wife and son, Stelios.

A lot of Greek Cypriots lived in the area. Mum would shop at "the Greek man" at his store on Seven Sisters Road. It was one of few places you could get Caribbean food. He stocked produce such as green bananas, sweet potatoes, and white or yellow yams. Every so often a friend would visit, having come from "back home" and bearing gifts of some mangoes or breadfruit, which we regarded as a rare and special treat. Whatever fruit they brought from the home country was always regarded as sweeter, tastier, and always superior to the same fruit if you could get it at the Greek man's shop.

## FIRST ENCOUNTERS

My mother recently told me that when I was in nursery school in the mid-1950s, she was constantly being told how bad her little three-year-old was. I reminisced with her about it. I was most likely the only Black child in the nursery school, which would be called pre-school today. An incident that occurred there is one of my earliest memories and mum filled in parts I had no idea about at the time.

I remember sitting on my little chair in the back row of a group of pre-schoolers. We were in a hall. The other children and I were seated in roughly three rows that only occupied a small part of the front of the hall. There was a big space behind me. The teacher sat in front facing us and it was perhaps story time. I can't remember that detail but I do remember pushing my chair back a little, then a little more, into the empty space behind me. I remember thinking she wouldn't notice as I gradually and stealthily pushed back. Mum recalls the staff constantly complaining about me and my mischievousness. On that day, they told my mother about this latest escapade of mine. Fed up with the constant barrage of complaints, mum asked them somewhat testily how one little three-year-old boy could cause them the amount of trouble they were reporting.

As I look back, I wonder whether I was that bad–or was I simply the object of the hyper scrutiny Black children face in relation to White authority? I really don't know for sure, but my experiences since then have made me unsure of their treatment of me in nursery school.

An experience I have no doubt about took place a few years later, in the early 1960s, while we were still living on Dunford Road. Playing with the White kids there was when I first heard commands such as, "Blackie, go home!" and "Go back to where you came from." We would play in a bombed-out section of the street at the end of a road adjacent to ours. It was just a pile of rubble. We played in and around it and we had fun but every now and then, I would be reminded of my place as an outsider and a stranger. Sometimes, they would call me "little Black Sambo"[1] or a "wog." I was an intruder. I didn't belong. The term wog came from a jam we used to buy made by James Robertson and Sons, Preserve Manufacturers Limited. Robertson's trademark was a golliwog, a blackface figure of a rag doll with white eyes. I had no idea of the childlike image of Black people that it caricatured at the time–nor did I, in my tender years, associate the term wog with Robertson's jam. All I knew was that if I were called a wog, it wasn't because people were being kind and friendly to me. On the contrary, it was an epithet hurled with venom.

My usual response was to ignore it as much as I could to prevent it from penetrating deep enough to hurt. In addition, I learned to not let my expression show in any way that the word wog had an effect on me. I would carry on regardless, implacable at least on the outside. I instinctively felt that showing the names hurt me would give those who spat them out a measure of control over me. They would sense weakness and increase their venom, using the names any time they wanted to inflict

---

1. "The name Sambo itself originates from the Spanish word *Zambo* used to describe a knock-kneed or cross-eyed person (Rout). Thus, Spain's racial history influences the nature of all *Little Black Sambo* books, the derogatory name used to describe a little black boy"; see "Spanish Sambo · Spectacular Blackness," WUSTL Digital Gateway Image Collections & Exhibitions, https://wayback.archive-it.org/org-786/20230327200026/http://omeka.wustl.edu/omeka/exhibits/show/spectacularblackness/little-black-sambo/spanish-sambo.

psychological pain on me. I also had a sense that dwelling on the hurt would hinder me from thriving in spite of the situation. I guess this is somewhat similar to what I've heard as a counsellor about the way firefighters and emergency medical service workers survive the horrible things they experience on a daily basis. Survival meant being implacable, not giving away any sense of fear or that it hurt.

I learned later that to survive slavery, my forebears were similarly implacable. To show fear or pain would give the slave owner even more control over you than they already had. If you were ever going to express your inner feelings, it would be among your own community who you loved and trusted. Of course, I now know that the drip effect of such attacks did indeed leave its mark. Thankfully, after Roberston's products were boycotted by Ken Livingston's Greater London Council in 1983, they dropped the trademark character from their advertising in 1988 due to its offensiveness.

I didn't like being treated that way. Still, it didn't appear to affect me that badly. I don't remember experiencing any anguish over it. I didn't go crying to my mum or dad, complaining about rejection; it was just part of the landscape. They were who they were, and I was who I was. I had been weighed in social balances and judged to be different. My skin colour and my nappy hair were Exhibits A and B.

If you had asked me about racism, even up to my teens I would have told you I personally didn't experience it. I had pushed those early experiences to the back of my mind. I was fine. I hadn't been subjected to some of the stuff I saw in newspapers or on television. What I *am* aware of, in hindsight, is that racism left its mark on my mind–a mark that manifested in my doodling, because I drew pictures of people who were exclusively White. The girls I drew had long flowing hair and none of the pictures I drew looked like me, my sisters (who now included Charlene and Caroline, respectively born in 1960 and 1964, in addition to Paula), or my parents. Deep down in the subconscious that I heard Dr. Pokorny at the Westminster Institute of Psychotherapy talk about in my counselling course there in later years, I didn't like myself. I was flawed. I was not desirable, beautiful, or acceptable in relation to a society that merely tolerated my presence.

Being strict Seventh-day Adventists, my parents didn't encourage me to associate too closely with the children on my street beyond playing nearby. Common to all people, my parents had their prejudices. Seventh-day Adventists believe they are special, chosen by God to fulfill a mission to bring people back to true worship, high standards of living, and respect for God. This provided an additional layer to their view of other people, even other Black people. Those kids used bad language. Their parents smoked. Their standards of hygiene were not as strict as ours. According to them, White people were "nasty." They wiped their children's smudged faces with a hankie and some spittle. They washed their dishes with soapy water and didn't rinse them afterwards. They licked their fingers when they were cooking and eating. So, I didn't go into their homes and hang out with them at all.

When I started going to primary school, I made friends there but

Photo of dad and mom taken in the late 1950s.

Photo of my family of origin. Pictured standing from left to right: my sisters, Charlene, Caroline, Paula, and Hymers Jr. (me). Seated on left with Sadiki, Paula's son on his lap is Hymers Sr. (dad) and on the right Dahlia (mom).

I recall visiting the home of one friend from school who lived around the corner just once. I was offered tea and found it revolting. We drank neither tea nor coffee–nothing with caffeine–at home. Maybe in a way, not associating too closely insulated me from any further feelings of not belonging. I don't recall getting visits welcoming us to the neighbourhoods we lived in, nor did I witness my parents having to turn down invitations pressing them to visit their White neighbours' homes.

## FOUNDATIONS FOR RESILIENCE

As with other West Indian parents in those days, our parents didn't like seeing us idle. If you were just around doing nothing, they would find a task for you to do or tell us, "Go read a book!"

My sister Paula and I joined the public library at Manor Gardens. We would walk together from Dunford Road heading northwest on Holloway Road past the Holloway Road tube station. We would pass under the bridge carrying the overground railway trains. Under the bridge was a public toilet, which later I learned had the reputation of being a hangout for men who used it to relieve their sexual urges. We would walk past the Beales department store, with its fashionable drapery and clothing, and the Marks & Spencer's clothing store. Just before crossing Seven Sisters Road, we would pass the Nags Head pub that was on the east side of Holloway Road and almost directly opposite the Holloway Seventh-day Adventist Church we attended on Saturdays. A short distance further and we'd be at Manor Gardens, where the library was opposite the Royal Northern Hospital.

My sister and I loved reading. My dad loved reading. My children love reading. Their mother loves reading. It's in our blood. I remember reading the Famous Five and Secret Seven books by Enid Blyton. As I got older, I discovered novels by Nevil Shute, particularly the book *A Town Like Alice*. Ernest Hemingway's books grabbed my attention. I was enthralled by *For Whom the Bell Tolls*, where I learned about the agonies and ecstasies of romance, love, and war. As I got older, my adolescent tastes turned to war stories. I especially loved reading about the exploits of the Royal Air Force fighter and bomber pilots and the laconic bravado with which they battled the Hun in the skies, first with their Hurricanes, Spitfires and Lancasters. My father had been in the Royal Air Force, so those stories meant even more to me by association.

On one of our journeys to the library, my sister and I did our usual thing of going our separate ways in the building to explore books of our liking. I found myself in the section where Ernest Hemingway's books were again. *The Old Man and the Sea* caught my attention and I picked it up to see whether I would like it. I started reading. Initially, the question in my mind was whether the book was interesting enough to take home. But like the giant marlin at the other end of aged Cuban fisherman Santiago's rod in the story, I was soon hooked. Pulled along by the plot, I kept turning page after page. I was transported onto the high seas of Cuba in those moments, oblivious to anything else. Santiago's struggle became my struggle. I kept reading, holding the book in my right hand up to my face as I stood beside the shelf that had yielded up that small piece of treasure. I read until I finished it, captivated by the account of strength and perseverance.

Finishing the book startled me. I had read the whole thing standing transfixed to the spot, my arm crooked so I could see the words. I had been standing in this position so long that my bicep ached and was almost completely frozen in place. I felt pain as I shook it out, extending, stretching, and bending my arm several times to get it functioning again. I was all too aware in that moment of the power of the written word and the ability of a wordsmith to paint a picture and drop their audiences, sometimes unwittingly, into the midst of places they never knew existed.

On another day, as my sister and I were heading back home from the library, each with the four books we were allowed to borrow for a couple of weeks in our hands, we saw a familiar sight. Identifiable by his rolling gait, a White man strode toward us muttering angrily, "Bloody Blacks and Cypriots." In the context of people calling us "niggers" (not infrequent in post-war England) and telling us to go back to where we came from, it was obvious that the presence of "bloody Blacks and Cypriots" in his community had gotten under his skin. He didn't stop to engage anyone. He just said these words angrily and loudly enough to be clearly heard, but as if he was having a conversation with himself. He stared straight ahead as he spoke. It would have been scary if he had stopped and aimed his vitriolic hatred at my sister and me directly, but he seemed to be in a world of his own. We had seen him enough times on Holloway Road to know that if he kept walking and we kept walking, taking care to avoid eye contact, he was harmless and we would be safe.

I had asked my parents about this man. They seemed to know who I was talking about, and they merely shrugged and said he was suffering from shellshock. Today, with all that has been written about post-traumatic stress disorder, which is apparently the new name for shellshock, I wonder if that man had been emotionally scarred by battle. Or had he simply been traumatized out of his rational mind by the Nazi blitzkrieg raining down bombs on civilians in North London a couple of decades previously? I speculate that perhaps the trauma had caused him to search for scapegoats for his plight and "bloody Blacks" and "Cypriots" fit the bill.

In addition to having my parents to turn to for help in navigating difficult encounters, a small number of uncles, aunts and cousins who formed our portion of the West Indian diaspora provided support and connections. My uncle Laurence Evelyn, my aunt Lorna Claire, and my cousins Fritz, Jerome and Paul, now known as Mamaniji, were closest to us. Uncle Evelyn had come back to the United Kingdom after his own stint in the Royal Air Force around the same time as my dad, also preparing the way for my aunt and cousins to come from Jamaica. Dad and his brother, my uncle Roston, and Uncle Evelyn, dad's brother-in-law, had roomed together on Ellington Street in North London back then, sometime between 1953 and 1954. Not too long after, we were joined by dad's sister, Aunt Alva Mowat, and her son Alfred, and Aunt Evadney, my mum's half-sister, together with her husband Keith Jackson and their daughter, Cousin Donna. Sometime later, Uncle Roston, the most eligible bachelor at the Holloway church–always impeccably dressed and supremely dapper–married Joyce Kennedy. Not too long after that, along came their daughter, Cousin Melanie. This was the extent of the extended family whose love surrounded my parents, sisters, and me. Their care, our mutual visits, the stories, and jokes about life 'back home' were like a bulwark against a society in which we all struggled to make our way.

I remember clearly a frightening incident in which Uncle Roston was mugged by Teddy Boys. With their distinctive flashy clothes and hairstyles, Teddy Boys were gangs of young White men who between the early 1950s and mid-1960s would randomly attack people–but most often targeted Black men in relationships with White women. Uncle Roston just happened to be in the wrong place at the wrong time coming home from work when a group of Teddy Boys accosted him and beat him up. We commiserated with him as we listened to his story and saw his bruised, scarred and battered face. It stunned me, but was no surprise. I had read reports of such attacks coupled with horrific photographs in the newspapers and had heard the terse news bulletins on the radio. I had heard about the Notting Hill race riot involving clashes between Teddy Boys and West Indian immigrants in West London in 1958. Black people were under attack and here was Uncle Roston, the latest victim, bringing the situation home to us in a more personal way.

It was a stark reminder that the streets of London could be dangerous for Black people, and we needed to be always wary and always on guard. Still, I never saw Uncle Roston wilt or shrink away because of that incident. His internal strength in dealing with the incident was a lesson to me about strength and fortitude in the face of rank adversity. I recalled this incident at a gathering of my extended family and friends recently. I wanted to let my adult children, cousins, and friends of the family know a little bit about the hardships our forebears endured to pave the way for us. We owed them a debt of gratitude and we owed it to them to emulate their courageous example. As I spoke to my extended family, I remembered how for Uncle Roston, life continued and he carried on living with characteristic humour, delighting family, friends, and church members with his beautiful voice ringing out the majestic song "The Holy City." Uncle Roston sang "Where E'er You Walk" at my wedding and as I recall the beautiful tenor voice of that Wilson patriarch, my tears flow freely.

Even with the loving extended family I had around me, I still felt something was missing. At school, I began to hear kids talking about "me nan" and "me grandad." My only knowledge of my grandparents was from what I was told about sitting on my granddad's knee as a baby before I left Jamaica, but I had no personal recollection of him nor of any of my other grandparents. As I reflect on this missing part of my experience, I can only wonder about the added dimension it could have brought to my life to have been able to interact with my grandparents and feel both their love and a sense of the enduring nature of our family. They might have given me a more personal connection to the history of our people, in particular the relatively recent history of the millions of people (including some of my ancestors) brought forcibly from Africa to work as slaves on Jamaican sugar plantations. My grandparents' parents would have known about slavery, perhaps hearing about it from people in their district in Jamaica who had felt its blight firsthand as former slaves themselves. They would have heard about how the slaves had to work from dawn to dusk under the unrelenting heat of the sun. They would also have heard about slaves being whipped for minor infractions and a harsh existence that produced an extremely high

Photo of dad's birth certificate showing grandparents names.

mortality rate.[2] At the same time, I probably would have heard from my grandparents how our forebears survived slavery.

I did, however, hear some stories about my grandparents. One was about how my paternal grandfather got his nickname as everybody in the family calls him T-H-E. When he was a young child in school, he was asked by the teacher to spell his name, which was Thomas. The request caught him off guard and flustered him momentarily. A mischievous boy behind him in the class, unseen and unheard by the teacher, whispered, "T-H-E." My hapless grandfather, relieved at his rescue from the peril of the all-too-common physical or possibly verbal retribution for missteps meted out by teachers in the West Indies in those days, repeated out loud for the benefit of the teacher and the class, "T-H-E." Knowing Jamaicans as I do, I can only imagine the side-splitting mirth

---

2. In his book about the history of the Caribbean between 1492 and 1969, Dr. Eric Williams writes, "In 1703 Jamaica had 45,000 Negroes; in 1778, 205,261 ... The total population in 1778 excluding births and based only on imports, should have been 541,893, and that figure excludes imports for 1776, 1777 and 1778 ... The actual population in that year was less than forty percent of the potential total"; see *From Columbus to Castro: The History of the Caribbean 1492–1969* (André Deutsch Limited, 1970), 146.

Photo of my grandfather Thomas (T-H-E) Wilson.

Photo of my grandmother, Mabel Wilson née Kerr.

this would have engendered, and the name T-H-E stuck to granddad like a limpet on a rock[3] to this day. This and other humorous stories gave me insight into an aspect of resilience of my people: the ability to find humour and laughter amongst the hardships of life.

Everyone having a pet or nickname is a feature of Jamaican culture that carried over into the diaspora. My nickname was Junior because I had the same name as my father. In the district where dad lived in Jamaica, there was Image Man, who was reputed to have seen a likeness of his own face carved into the trunk of a tree and exclaimed, "Nuh me dat?" In one of the churches my dad attended in the United Kingdom, there was a short man they called Quarter Man. In a church I pastored in later years, there was Brother Easy (whose real name was Hardy). My cousin Dwight was called Fritz. In formal work settings, Uncle Evelyn was Laurence or Larry. My cousin Clarence called my mother D, short for Dahlia, her first name. Aunt Evadney was called Niecie. Each name started either as a description of some humorous event the person had been involved in or something about their physical attributes–or was simply preferred. It was the same with grandfather. We don't call T-H-E "Tom" or "Thomas." The family wouldn't know who you were talking about if you did.

My small extended family in the United Kingdom, the culture and values we shared along with the humour and dignified strength with

---

3. "Common limpets are the small cone-like shells that are often seen firmly clamped to the side of rocks in rockpools. Although they may not look impressive at first glance, once the tide comes in they spring to action, moving around rocks eating algae using their tough tongue. Their tongue is the world's strongest known biological structure–it needs to constantly scrape algae off of tough rocks!" ("Common Limpet," The Wildlife Trusts, https://www.wildlifetrusts. org/wildlife-explorer/marine/sea-snails-and-sea-slugs/common-limpet).

which they faced life, were the invaluable underpinnings of my early life. They provided me with the resilience I relied on to navigate the murky pathways leading through school, college, university, and employment in my later years.

## CHURCH LIFE

Church was the place where I formed more intimate friendships with people who weren't biological family. Here were people of like minds. Here were Black children like me.

I started attending the Holloway Seventh-day Adventist Church from the time we arrived fresh off the boat. The term 'fresh off the boat' has been used consistently ever since to describe a recent immigrant from the Caribbean. It carried connotations of a person who presented as awkwardly trying to fit in with the new culture, a person who dressed in bright colours that wouldn't have looked strange in the islands but contrasted with the dull colours worn in post-war England. That person spoke with a pronounced accent and with broken English that we, who grew up as children in England, called "green verbs." They were like what the English would call 'country bumpkins' and the Jamaicans 'country bookies.' Now, every new immigrant from the islands arrives by airplane but they continue to be referred to as 'fresh off the boat.'

At the time I arrived in England by boat, the Holloway church we attended was mostly White but by the time I left for college it was almost one hundred percent Black. Church increasingly became a place of refuge where I associated with young Black people. It was a place where we laughed together, prayed together, listened to uplifting messages, and played together. We were in church on a Saturday morning, went home after the service ended at about 12:20 p.m., and had a sumptuous 'Sabbath' dinner–always the best dinner of the week. Then we would go back in the afternoon for a youth meeting that the adults came to as well. After the youth meeting and following sunset, we would have youth club, which could last until 10 o'clock or even 11 o'clock at night.

Church was a place where I and my Black friends would take comfort from the knowledge that we might be strangers in a strange land, but a better, brighter day was coming. This world was not our final resting place. We used to sing a particular gospel song in characteristic bouncy, catchy Southern gospel style that cemented this sentiment firmly and unshakeably within us:

This world is not my home
I'm just a-passing through
My treasures are laid up
Somewhere beyond the blue

The angels beckon me
From heaven's open door
And I can't feel at home
In this world anymore

Oh Lord, you know
I have no friend like you
If heaven's not my home,
Then Lord, what will I do?

The angels beckon me
From heaven's open door,
And I can't feel at home
In this world anymore[4]

We were just passing through; heaven was our goal. For the growing Black membership, this meant that whatever the 'Man' (our word for the system) threw at us, we could shake it off and carry on regardless. We had each other and we had God on our side. Even before the civil rights mantras of "I'm Black and I'm beautiful" and the singer James Brown's "Say it loud–I'm Black and I'm proud," we were reminded over and over that we were children of God and heirs of greater things to come.

I remember a Black preacher, Pastor H. S. Walters, came to visit our church from Jamaica. Up to that time, the church had been served exclusively by White ministers. Here was this preacher of dark skin and imposing stature, preaching with a conviction and power like nothing I had heard before. He preached with his whole body, moving back and forth across the platform like he owned it. His expression was fiery. His eyes flashed as he fixed his gaze on the congregation with a challenge to live our lives in harmony with a forgiving and loving God. It was different. The experience convicted me that what he was offering, in terms of a connection with almighty God, was what I needed to help me get through life. This was one of a series of pivotal moments where I decided that Christianity offered me strength, comfort, and a sense of belonging to something

---

4. "This World Is Not My Home," Timeless Truths, accessed January 8, 2025, https://library. timelesstruths.org/music/This_World_Is_Not_My_Home/.

greater than myself. Part of that conviction, I'm sure, had to do with the fact that I was seeing a successful Black man who was eloquent. He didn't use 'green verbs'; his command of the English language was superlative. He was impeccably dressed. He was a role model.

## WHITE FLIGHT

Within a few short years of our arrival, my dad became the first Black elder at the Holloway Seventh-day Adventist Church. Dad was well known in the Seventh-day Adventist denomination in the 1950s and beyond. He was featured in a television program called *The Saturday People* along with Denis Uffindell and another Adventist. We used to have black and white pictures at home taken in the 1950s of dad smiling and happy with White church members, mostly women. If you visit the church today, you'd be hard pressed to find even a single White member. Racism has cast its shadow, even into the hallowed sanctuary of the church.

I began to hear about so-called White flight when the vast majority of the congregation was still White. Bit by bit, the White members started disappearing. The young ones left first. I remember the Guenin brothers, Roland and Louis, who became a dentist. I don't know where they went. There was no farewell or fanfare. They just vanished as far as I was aware. Later, their father and mother left after Mr. Marcel Guenin was voted out of his position as head elder of the church. And today, the Holloway church is a Black church with a large contingent of African members who followed the earlier influx of members from the Caribbean.

At first, we pulled our hair out, so to speak, trying to figure out what we could do to attract White people back to church. We wanted to show that the Christian gospel message, particularly the Seventh-day Adventist brand, had irrefutable appeal to all races. We distributed leaflets talking about the gospel and last day events to people in the areas surrounding the church. The gospel referred to the good news that Jesus could save humanity from greed, famine, wars, and disease, to name a few of its woes. Last day events were a reference to the Seventh-day Adventist belief in the Second Coming of Jesus signalling the end of the world as we know it and the climactic events, including persecution of believers in God, leading up to it. We held meetings inviting friends, neighbours, and workmates to attend–but to no avail. The problem seemed to be us. Our Blackness appeared to be a hindrance, an obstacle.

I thought this way for a long time until it became apparent to me that the problem wasn't with us. We worshipped with anybody. We were accepting of all ethnicities. It became clear that it was the Whites who had the problem associating with Black members. This was a liberating thought. We could cast off the burdensome idea of it being our fault that Whites didn't want to fellowship with us.

In the same way, I was able to rationalize a scary incident I experienced when I was about 12 years old. I was riding my bike pedalling southwest along Seven Sisters Road. I was on my way back from visiting my three boy cousins who lived in Tottenham, home of the famous Tottenham Hotspurs soccer club. I was riding on the pavement or sidewalk closest to the Finsbury Park fence toward Hornsey Road where I would take a left passing my old school, Pakeman Primary, to get home.

Two teenage boys on the back of a small engine motorbike travelling in the same direction zoomed up beside me. "Blackie, go home!" the one on the back yelled out, and he spat at me. They rode alongside me for a moment, hurling their epithets at me. I was paralyzed, not knowing what would happen next. Then, they suddenly zoomed off leaving me behind, my legs quivering with fear.

Many years later, I thought about that incident and reflected on the hatred those teenage boys had for a young defenceless boy they knew nothing about simply because he was Black. I rationalized that *I* was okay. There was nothing wrong with *me*. *They* were the ones with the problem, having such poisonous ideas running through their minds. I have told this story many times in counselling to my clients, especially to those with low self-esteem who have internalized the perceived negativity of others toward them. I hoped to help them reframe their experiences of other people's snubs, placing the problem firmly back where it belonged.

This mindset helped me be resilient and push the dark shadow of racism away, preventing me from becoming overly burdened and emotionally stunted by its negative messages. I could see myself as being okay. My self-esteem was intact. I reasoned that people who voiced racist language were damaged in some way. They needed an honest understanding of history, how we West Indians came to be in England, and the contributions we had made to life in Britain both in the past and in the present.

# SCHOOL DAYS
## Primary School

From age five or six to age 10, I attended Pakeman Primary School on Hornsey Road. There was only one other Black kid there, a boy called Newton. He was always in trouble. My mum told me recently that the teachers had advised her to keep me away from him so I wouldn't be affected by his waywardness. I didn't know this at the time. Apart from Newton, there was one other visible minority kid at the school that I remember. His name at the time was Manin Kelly. In January 2015, we connected by chance on LinkedIn. He told me that after leaving Pakeman Primary, he attended Tollington Grammar School in Muswell Hill and then joined the Royal Air Force at 17 years old as an apprentice Air Radar Technician working on C-130 Transport Planes. After some years, he joined the Sultan of Oman's Air Force in 1974 where he began flying fighters. He subsequently flew commercial flights in 1980. He now goes by the impressive name Manin Bin Khalifa Al-Said.

I have good memories of Pakeman Primary School. My first teacher there was Miss Brownjohn. My last teacher in the primary school was Miss Hatton, a former ballerina. This was evident in her tall, regal-like bearing. The expression "empty vessels make the most noise," which she often used to say, stuck with me. One particularly fond memory I have is from when I was introduced to country dancing at around 8 years old. Miss Hatton asked all of the children in my age group to choose a partner; we had been gathered in a group and left to pair up. I made a beeline for Susan Waller. Precociously romantic, I was in love with her as much as an 8-year-old could be. Much to my enduring delight, she was open to being paired with me and this made my day.

In fact, she made my final two years at Pakeman Primary School an absolute dream. We practiced country dancing together and went to country dancing festivals where representatives from other schools would strut their stuff. I had a whale of a time, learning and executing the steps with precision and twirling around that beautiful girl. It made no difference to us that she was White and I was Black. I saw her once after leaving that school a few years later, when our family had moved to Ronalds Road in Highbury. We exchanged "hellos" and other polite pleasantries, but that was it. I regret, with all my heart, losing touch with her after that.

As I think about my time at Pakeman Primary School, perhaps the fun I had country dancing obscured the shadow of racism, that ever-present companion. Yet as I reflect more deeply and wave away the haze that obscures distant negative memories, I recall something unsettling that happened in Miss Lacey's class. She was a gruff, single woman with grey stubble on her chin and lipstick applied somewhat haphazardly on her lips. She was called 'Miss' Lacey because, as with most female teachers in the 1950s and 1960s, she was single. I was sitting at my desk not quite on the back row on the right side of the room facing her. All of the pupils were quietly working at their desks as those were the days when silence in class was strictly enforced.

I felt a sudden urge to go to the toilet. I raised my hand to get the teacher's attention, as the rules demanded. Miss Lacey eventually saw my hand.

"Yes?"
"May I go to the toilet, Miss Lacey?"
"No, you may not."

I was devastated. I was dying to pee. I sat at my desk, bewildered by the refusal to allow me to empty my bladder. I sat and tried to contain the urgency. Then suddenly, I couldn't hold it any longer and out it came, forming a puddle under my desk and chair. Now, I had another problem: what to do about the puddle under my desk. I got some blotting paper and started to soak up as much of the urine as I could. The pupil next to me noticed what I was doing and asked what the matter was. I mumbled something about water from rain or a spill. My deskmate started helping me to soak up the 'water' with his blotting paper. Just then, our efforts were interrupted by Miss Lacey calling me to where she was sitting at her desk facing the class.

"Hymers Wilson, come here." She was scowling with displeasure. When I got to her desk on her left side, she pointed angrily at my exercise book in front of her where she had been marking my arithmetic. "This is wrong," she said, face contorted with disapproval at my numeracy failures. The next thing I knew, she was throwing my exercise book clear to the back of the classroom with her right hand and spanking me on my backside with her left. What her left hand encountered there totally surprised her. She held it up and stared at it. Her face now took on a look of disbelief and disgust as the realization of her hapless contact with my urinary mishap broke through the initial fog of confusion about the wet sensation on her hand.

Just then, I was literally saved by the bell as it sounded for the end of class. I don't know how that embarrassing debacle in the classroom ended. All I remember is that I ran home as fast as I could because it was lunchtime and got a change of clothes from my mother. I also recall that my father, who quite distinctly had given the teachers permission on my first day at school to spank me if I misbehaved, went to the school to remonstrate with Miss Lacey about her ill-advised actions that day.

Was I treated that way because I was Black? It's hard to say, but that's the thing about racism. I look back and wonder about those kinds of incidents and think about why other children weren't refused permission to go to the toilet when they put their hands up and asked to do so. Why don't I recall any other children being spanked for getting their sums wrong? I was a bright child. In July 1961, Miss Brownjohn wrote on my school report that "Hymers has made steady progress throughout the year and his work is always neatly and well done." Miss Hatton's comment on my July 1963 school report was "Hymers has done a good year's work. He has ability." I even passed my Eleven Plus exam, which allowed me the privilege of attending a grammar school, a school for more gifted pupils–a step up from the secondary modern schools–when I left primary school.

So I ask myself why, when I got to grammar school, I tended to sit toward the back of my classes and why I chose to act as the class clown and mimic teachers, much to the considerable delight of my classmates.

## GRAMMAR SCHOOL

At the end of my time in primary school, in approximately 1963, we moved to 55 Ronalds Road in Highbury. Our family had our own house at last. From an early age, I had caught my parents' frustration with living in rented accommodation. Landlords would impose restrictions on how we could decorate and living as a tenant with other families would inevitably lead to (often petty) conflicts. As children, we were constantly on guard about being too loud and making noise that would cause the tenants downstairs to knock on their ceiling with a broom handle to express their displeasure. There was, however, a glitch with our house. My parents had bought it with the understanding that it came with a sitting tenant, an elderly lady who lived on the third floor. By law, she couldn't be moved and so there she remained for a number of years.

It was from Ronalds Road that I attended Owens Grammar School for Boys from age 10 to 19 (1963 to 1972). There were only two other Black pupils there in my year. I think we were among the first few Black children at Owens back then. One of them was in my class–Georgie Lee, as we called him. The other, Alan Hunter, was in another class of the same age group. I enjoyed being at school; I enjoyed the camaraderie and the jokes we boys told each other. It was fun going to school and playing football (called soccer in North America) in the quad, as the playground was known. We were divided in our loyalties to a large extent between those boys who supported Arsenal Football Club and the Tottenham Hotspurs Football Club. However, the rivalry wasn't that serious. One of my friends, Alan Droy, had a brother, Mickey, who was somewhat of a celebrity because he was good enough at football to play for Tottenham. I hung out with Alan, Robert Harness, Phillip Woolway, and my closest friend Vincent Sartori, to name a few.

Enjoying friendship with the boys, playing football and cricket in the quad with them at recess and lunchtime, was my focus throughout my first few years at Owens. These were sweaty encounters played in our school uniforms minus our blazers, which we lay down to mark out

**Owen's School – Class of '64 (1 D.R. Neal)**
[Colourised by Les Gibbings [Back Row, 4th Right]

The author at 11 years old pictured on the front row, third from the left of the Dame Alice Owen's Grammar School for Boys class of '64 photo.

goal posts. Almost the whole school played in the confined space of the quad, each group (usually clustered by age) carving out their space to play games in which there were good-natured winners and losers.

When it was our turn to go for the school dinners cooked on the premises, we would descend to the dinner hall soaking from our exertions. Famished, we were relieved to eat lamb chops, mashed potatoes, pork sausages, Yorkshire pudding, and other typically English culinary delights. The meals were completed with dessert we called Afters, such as spotted dick, treacle pudding, apple crumble, hot custard, and other such treats served up by the dinner ladies. School dinners cooked on premises are now a thing of the dim and distant past. I enjoyed those meals in spite of English schoolboy songs poking fun at them, such as the song we sang mischievously,

"Say what you will, school dinners make you ill. Davy Crockett died of shepherd's pie. All school din-dins come from pig bins out of town ... "

Not only was I one of the boys singing mischievous songs, but my position as class clown had come entrenched and I was having great fun imitating and ridiculing teachers. I speculate now–and it's just a feeling, an intuition–that on some level, I wasn't sensing a caring warmth and recognition from the authority figures (namely, the teachers). This was perhaps my way of getting the recognition I craved from my fellow pupils. I don't recall being punished for it but it began to be reflected in my grammar school reports. In July 1967, one of my form or home room teachers wrote, "Ever since he came to Owens, his reports have been witness to the fact that he has ability but he is inattentive in class and does not work hard enough." Despite passing my Eleven Plus exam and despite ending my first year of grammar school with reasonable marks, my academic performance was deteriorating.

I didn't experience mentoring by any teacher in those days. No one took me aside, expressing an interest in seeing me improve. Perhaps that's just the way things were back then: it was sink or swim. If you understood subject matter quickly and you were able to produce good work, you advanced. Mathematics was particularly challenging for me until my parents got me a tutor, Charles Balcombe, from Guyana, who patiently explained the concepts I needed to know. Brother Balcombe, a tall, handsome Black man who was also a member of my local church, was himself working on his PhD in inorganic chemistry. He had formulae on sheet after sheet of paper, wall to wall in his humble apartment situated next door to the Arsenal Football stadium where he lived with his wife Beryl. It was clearly a language he had mastered. Thanks to his tutelage, I passed my mathematics O Level much to my, and no doubt his, delight.

I reflected on that time in my teenage years after experiencing, many years later, the mentorship of Dr. Cheryl Regehr, with whom I took three classes at Wilfrid Laurier University when I was in my forties. She liked my work and the grades I achieved with her were stellar. But what spurred me on to excel even more was her taking me aside and encouraging me to do a PhD through the University of Toronto in their sociology department. I never did follow up on her suggestion, but I have never forgotten how affirming it felt to have a professor take a personal interest in my academic performance for the first time in my life. I graduated from Wilfrid Laurier with a Master of Social Work with distinction.

My academic performance in my first years at Owens was far from one of distinction. I was just having a lot of fun that was punctuated by the dreaded experience of bringing my school report home at the end of each school year for the attention of my father. He would invariably get angry with me for my dismal performance. For my part, I would feel severely chastened. It was understood in our community that in order to get ahead in English society, one had to be at least better than–ideally, twice as good as–White people. Because this is what I heard so often, to this day, if I see a Black person who has risen to the top in the corporate world, government, or politics, I highly suspect it is because they were either a genius or they worked harder or achieved twice as many positive results as their counterparts. Having to be twice as good was a pressure I felt most keenly at those times when my report was shared with my parents. I would resolve to do better next school year but as with many resolutions, messing about with my friends made my resolve dissipate until I reached the fifth form. It was then that I decided it was do or die; I had to make a change in my academic trajectory.

I determined that my time was better spent working on my assignments in the library at lunch time instead of frittered away in the quad playing soccer. So there I was in the library one lunchtime, working on my assignment. I wasn't aware of anything going on around me until a master, one of the teachers, burst into the library area, complaining about the noise in the room and pointing an accusatory finger at me, the only Black boy in the room. He had quickly identified me as the guilty party. To him, I was naturally the one responsible for the forbidden chatter in the room. I remember feeling especially aggrieved because I had been making a sincere effort to get my work done. I imagined my reputation as a mischief maker garnered in previous years allowed that teacher to swiftly judge the situation he encountered in the library that day. But I wonder whether his arrival at a conclusion before he knew the facts was a decision bolstered by prejudice or merely my reputation as a mischief maker.

## THE SHADOWY INTERLOPER

The history I was taught at Owens from age 10 to 14 stealthily slipped elements of the shadow companion into my subconscious. Given the way they were presented to my young mind I couldn't possibly see the exploits of the so-called Virgin Queen, Elizabeth I, for what they really were. I just remember accounts of brave men such as Sir Francis Drake, sanctioned by the Queen to explore the New World and fight against the Spanish. How was I to know he was little more than a mercenary hired by his queen to be the vanguard of a colonizing contender? I cringed whenever sanitized snippets of the slave trade were divulged in class to impressionable ears. Britain was truly great–a master of the high seas subduing India, Africa, the Arab world, and the Caribbean, where I was born. I was thus part of the subdued; my forebears were the hapless victims of European force of arms and ingenuity. My people needed to be civilized. We needed to be rescued from animism and worship of wood and stone.

I kept my head down when these subjects came up in class, embarrassed and ashamed. I wish I could tell you I stood up and argued with the version of history I was being fed. I have heard that some Black children find their voices in those situations, but it wasn't so with me. I just wanted those classes to be over. I wanted to shut the history book with their images of resplendent British lords, ladies, and military officers pictured in stark contrast to the natives wherever they were found. No mention was made of the grand and glorious history of Africa, India, Arabia, and places in between. I wanted to escape to the quad and have a fun game of football with the lads and push the intrusion of the shadowy interloper deeper into the recesses of my mind. I could perform on the quad. I could dribble the ball, score a few goals, and go in hard with a tackle or two to establish that I was no pushover. I could be tough. No one picked on me as I could handle myself. I was somehow different from those images of my people that I saw in those history books.

At church, there was a twin assault on my subconscious—one just as shadowy and just as stealthy. Every Saturday morning in church, prior to the main (or what we called "the divine") service, we had Sabbath School. In this part of the day, we had a brief program featuring a hymn that we all sang together, a reading from the Bible, and a brief exhortation to be good Bible students or just good people. Then we had Bible study, which was when the church divided up into classes. Bible study was followed by the Mission Story, and this is where the shadowy interloper made its subtle assault. In the Mission Story, we were regaled with stories of missionaries taking the gospel to benighted—mostly Black, Brown, and sometimes Yellow—people who were "in darkness." The words with which they were described would be an affront in today's world, which has skilfully removed the language while maintaining the perspective that people with White skin are inherently superior. Grown Black men and women in Australasia were referred to as "Fuzzy-Wuzzies," as though they were cute little children.

Yet at the same time, I began to be exposed to a different reality primarily by way of the civil rights movement in America. The slogan "Black is beautiful!" in the mouth of Dr. Martin Luther King, Jr., awakened a sense of pride in my blackness. Hearing Jesse Jackson's repetition of "I am…somebody!" stirred me. Yes, I could hold my head up! I could love myself. I might be called hurtful, derogatory names by the ill-informed people I encountered, but role models such as King and Jackson were building on the foundation laid by my parents that I was loved, respected, and a person of worth. I even drew strength from Malcolm X, seen by many as a dangerous firebrand who spouted angry rhetoric, calling on Black people to fight back against oppression in complete contrast to King's message of non-violent resistance to racism. Malcolm X was in his way strengthening my father's example, in his wartime encounters, of having backbone and not being a pushover. I held these two ideas of non-violent and violent resistance in a strange tension in my mind. Alongside positive messages about my Blackness, they helped me to survive and thrive.

Despite this encouragement, I still had to contend with situations that left me with feelings of not belonging. One of these came when I was about 18 years old and school was over for the summer holidays. I had been looking for summer employment but didn't have a job yet and I needed money, so I decided to "go on the dole" and get the unemployment benefit. I went to the local social security office. When it was my

Photo in my late teens with full afro identifying with the Black is Beautiful slogan of the Civil Rights movement.

turn to go up to the official to find out how to apply, she asked me a question that floored me.

"Where are you from?"

I was shocked. I had grown up in England. I had come from Jamaica when I was one year old, so I didn't even speak English with a Jamaican accent. I had attended a prestigious English grammar school. England was my home and I had no other. I wasn't expecting a sharp inquiry from an official who had immediately identified me as "other." I was getting a message that I didn't belong. I may have assumed England was my home, but the official had other ideas that shattered my assumptions as a rock shatters a pane of glass into a thousand irreparable pieces.

What further contributed to my distress was that at the time, I had a Jamaican passport. I got it when I was sixteen years old and needed one to take a trip to Switzerland for a youth congress organized by the Seventh-day Adventist Church. I saw myself as Jamaican because I had been born in Jamaica to Jamaican parents. Yet while I was proud to be Jamaican, I had no experience of life there. The reality of my situation was that England was all I knew and the situation forced me to confront that reality head-on for the first time. I began to ask myself questions about where I belonged. Was Jamaica my real home, or was it England?

My Jamaican passport photo taken at 16 years old.

The official in the social security office thus introduced a sense of doubt and apprehension about my status into my mind. I managed to get my dole money but the experience of applying for it had shaken any illusions I had about acceptance in my adopted home, my country. It propelled me without much hesitation to apply for British citizenship immediately afterwards in order to get a British passport. No one was going to dislodge me from my home. I was in England to stay.

Some months ago, prior to the time of writing this, I learned that people from the Caribbean who had come to England as babies and young children—people like me—were being deported back to the Caribbean. They were being sent back because they had no certificates of citizenship, no British passports. The so-called Windrush Generation (those who had come over to England with their parents on a boat called the Windrush in 1948 as well as other boats like it, and who hadn't applied for citizenship) were being kicked back by the British Home Office to the countries from which their parents had brought them. I, for example, had been pictured on my mother's British passport held in her arms. But we were British subjects, not citizens—a distinction whose implications escaped many. British subjects were not automatically granted the right of abode in the United Kingdom and somehow the children of those British subjects fell afoul of a scandalous desire of vote-hungry politicians to appease their base by agitating for deportation.

The incident I experienced in the social security office somehow awakened in my young mind a presentiment of just such a deportation scenario five decades later. It had somehow presented me with the very

Photo of my mom and I in our first British Subject passport.

real possibility of being told to go back to a "home" I did not know. I realized then and there the importance of taking all available steps to make sure I was accepted as an equal in England. People like that official in the social security office could have their doubts about my status because of the colour of my skin but on paper, I would have legal proof that I belonged as much as any other British citizen.

A few years later, I got an answer to the question I had asked myself in the social security office about whether Jamaica was my real home. It was 1975 and I was in Jamaica for my cousin Fritz's wedding. It was the first time I had been back since mum had taken me with her to meet up with dad for his first encounter with his new baby. One morning, my cousin Fritz (Dwight) and I went for a jog in the stadium in Kingston.

A local soccer team was training there. I overheard one of the players saying, "Watch a de two White bwoy dem."

I couldn't believe my ears. My cousin, whose complexion could easily be mistaken for mixed race or biracial, and I, a few shades darker, were being referred to as White boys! I was seen as a stranger here in Jamaica as well. I was confounded, baffled, and befuddled. In my mind, my decision a few years earlier to cement my British citizenship was well and truly vindicated.

With the summer over, it was back to school and one last kick at the can. The urgency to achieve academically was foremost in my mind as my parents' words rang continuously in my ears: "you have to do twice as good as the Whites to get ahead." The reality was that I was not doing twice as good as anybody at that point. I was desperately trying my hardest to get three Cs in my advanced-level General Certificates of Education (or GCE A Levels). Humber University was offering me a spot to do law if I got them. Unfortunately, I had no idea of my learning style. Looking back, I realize now that I studied without a system. I spent long hours staring at books but not knowing how to assimilate the information in a way that I could recall for exams later. I didn't have a mentor or a guidance counsellor to advise me like they have today in my current home country, Canada. If I had, I likely would have discovered sooner how to translate my natural academic abilities into what the school system required of me.

Exams were the bane of my life. I took too long to answer questions and it felt like I was being tested on speed of producing answers more than anything else. I couldn't recall what I had learned in the time allotted, so I didn't get the three Cs I needed. Humber University, the prospect of a law degree, and a career as a barrister or solicitor became a mirage. Today, I live vicariously through my son, Hymers III, who graduated with a Juris Doctor (JD) degree, passed his bar exam, and was called to the bar. With law no longer an option for me, I would have to keep looking for where I belonged in the world of work.

## FIRST TASTE OF FULL-TIME EMPLOYMENT

The day I left school, I trekked across the road to an employment agency with about five other schoolmates. I tell what happened next with some degree of nostalgia. We were all looking at jobs in London where the stockbroking offices were. All five of us boys got jobs that very day! That's the nostalgia part. We all walked out of that employment agency with information about where to report for our jobs. As far as I know, this is something unheard of today.

I wore a suit and tie to my job at Montagu Loebl Stanley at 19 Throgmorton Avenue, City of London. I looked the part of the young man finding his way in the heart of the British financial establishment. Here I was in this august firm established in 1885, a British bastion. There was a new language to learn, older Englishmen to understand. There was the "Good morning, Reggie" in cultured middle-class cadences each morning. My cockney accent acquired in the spaces of Owens Grammar School for Boys over seven years disappeared, and I became just as cultured in my new role as a junior stockbroker. There was the Dickensian layout of the room where I worked, with desks in rows and

White men hunched over doing endless (and for me, mindless) calculations of stock prices.

It didn't take long for my ethereal companion to rear its nebulous
head. It happened in a flurry of excited activity. One day, I was sitting
at my desk adding up numbers–a task I performed like the game involving
a blindfolded child pinning a tail to a donkey. I became conscious of a
stir to my left, where the entrance to the room was at the back of the
office. A bright-faced young man was being welcomed. I listened in as
the older men greeted him. Then, I heard the young man bring them up
to date on a recent achievement. He had gotten into stockbroking college.
The greetings turned to congratulations and pats on the back. He received
the affirmation of a favourite son.

The incident left a profound impression on me. I had questions.
Why had I not heard about stockbroking college? I had no idea such
colleges with such specific training existed. Where was it? How did
one get accepted to such a college? Why had the men I worked with
not mentioned it to me? Why did *I* not feel the warmth of the emotional
embrace of the men around me? This is the part that is painful for me
because it exposes my inability to navigate this part of my journey
successfully. I could have asked questions about the college. In fact,
I probably would have become a successful stockbroker and I would
have liked that. Hymers Wilson, stockbroker, with a career arc that
would have led to a house in Surrey in the pristine English countryside.

Instead, I had psyched myself out because of my shadow companion.
I didn't feel like I belonged. It appeared to me then that the only way

I'd be able to get ahead would be to chart my own course. I'd find a college or university myself. I'd launch myself into a career. I'd find within myself the strong ability to be independent and self-motivated. I wouldn't have an ally in the next part of my journey. My parents had none of the skills or advantages needed to guide me as neither had reached my level of education. They didn't have the experience of navigating post-secondary education. They were too busy trying to survive themselves, preoccupied with maintaining the achievement of an immigrant family owning their own home and providing for my three younger sisters. I had been to a good school and as far as they were concerned, I had been taught what I needed to make my way in the world.

I left Montagu Loebl Stanley after a few months. I had lost my way somewhat and felt that I wasn't going to get anywhere if I stayed there. I knew I had to acquire more education. That was at least one positive thing my parents had given me, apart from a stable home and a faith in God. But it was about the end of April 1972 and colleges already had their cohorts for that school year. I went instead to a job I had worked previously, during school holidays, at the Department of Health and Social Security (DHSS). Arthur Torrington, a civil servant there at the time, was working as an executive officer and had helped me get jobs there in the past. So, here I was again. Arthur was originally from Guyana and has become well-known in the United Kingdom for his work on telling the Windrush story.

I found myself again churning out milk stamps for mothers on welfare in a smoke-filled room. There were no government health warnings about cigarettes or smoking bans in those days. I lasted two months there in May and June of 1972 before the lure of visiting my cousins in Boston, Massachusetts, and the £60 return student airfare from London Heathrow Airport to JFK in New York with Trans World Airlines snagged me.

Finding where I belonged in the world of work would have to wait.

## AMERICAN EYE-OPENER

I spent two glorious months in Jamaica Plain, Boston. My cousins Fritz, Paul, and Jerome had emigrated there from England a few years earlier. I used to hang out with them when they lived in Tottenham, North London, England. We played pick-up games of football (soccer) at Markfield Park and ate sumptuous meals prepared by their mother, my aunt Claire. Now in the United States, it was a time of reunion. It was fascinating to see how Americanized they had become. I was introduced to words such as "guy" and "homey dude."

But my trip to the States wasn't all positive. My first jarring experience confronted me as my bus out of JFK as it got on its way to the major roads to Boston. It would become another reminder of the ubiquity of the shadow.

I sat on the bus as it wound its way out of New York City. What I saw shocked me. I had been brought up on a sanitized diet of American life as seen in the movies. I remember seeing little blond girls with pigtails and bright blue-eyed boys on American television running into huge, well-equipped kitchens yelling, "Mommy! Mommy! I'm hungry, I'm hungry!" and then sitting down with huge glasses of orange juice.

Not only was the idea of running into a kitchen with an expectation of my hunger being immediately satisfied foreign to me, but I had never seen glasses that big before. Then there was the size of the apple one happy child was given: it was as big as a grapefruit one could buy at Sainsbury's. It seemed everything was bigger and better in America. Hollywood convinced me that the houses were bigger, the food more plentiful, and the cars more powerful.

But the sight that now met my eyes had me confused. I passed block after block of drab, grey housing. People–Black people–were sitting on what I learned later were called stoops. They didn't appear to be doing much else other than sitting there, watching the world from the steps in front of their houses. They looked lethargic. I didn't see any manicured lawns. There were no tree-lined boulevards. Frankly, it was a very depressing sight and a few miles of that concrete landscape decimated the myths I had grown up with. This was a part of America I had never seen in the movies. I'm not saying it didn't exist in the movies; it's just that I had never noticed it.

I asked myself why those neighbourhoods look so impoverished. Why was it that I only saw Black people sitting on those steps? Why did I not get the impression of a happy energy about the place? The questions didn't linger as concrete soon gave way to highways and open fields. I could breathe again and my attention turned to the anticipation of seeing my cousins. But later in life, I got my answer to the question of why those areas existed when I read about the practice of red-lining ("denying services, loans, or jobs to certain residents of certain areas"), which "helped to lock the Black underclass into inner cities decimated by cutbacks in federal aid"[5] in America. This was a practice I encountered in the United Kingdom and even a cursory Google search reveals that happened in Canada as well.

When I got off the bus in Jamaica Plain, Boston, I remember walking toward Dalrymple Street where my three cousins, my aunt Claire, and my uncle Evelyn lived. Uncle Evelyn, whose full name was Laurence Evelyn Crichton, was called Larry by the Americans. I had come to America for the first time. With an ear keenly attuned to accents from an early age, I listened for American ones. To the British ear in those days, the American accent was cool. After all, it was the accent of success and power. I had a friend in London who had never set foot in America but because of his hero worship of Muhammad Ali, he cultivated an American accent such that people who didn't know his origins routinely asked where in America he was from.

It was hot and humid walking towards my uncle and aunt's home with Fritz, one of my cousins who had met me in New York. People were out on the streets, calling to each other. The music in their houses leaked out onto the street. There were more surprises: I heard Jamaican accents and Caribbean beats regaling the neighbourhood. I didn't hear a single American accent.

There are some things you never forget, even with the passage of time. Though it's been nearly 50 years and much has been forgotten of what I experienced that summer in Boston, there is one horrific scene I

---

5. Henry Louis Gates, Jr. and Donald Yacovone, *The African Americans: Many Rivers To Cross* (SmileyBooks, 2013), 255.

can still see far too vividly in my mind that nothing has been able to erase. Literally just a few steps from where my cousin lived, a Black man had been apprehended by two police officers. The buzz in the neighbourhood was that he had gone through a red light. The police were ordering him to put his hands up. The man was complying but asking what he had done wrong. Just then, two other police officers pulled up in another cruiser. Seeing them arriving and apparently embold-ened by the backup, one of the original officers pulled out his gun. I had never, ever in my life seen a gun pulled in public in front of me and I have never, ever seen this since. The scene unfolded: another police officer pulled out his baton and started beating the Black man over the head until his stick burst a blood vessel. Now, blood streamed down the Black man's face. There was nothing shadowy about this confrontation.

The Black man was taken away by the police. I was shaken to the core by the incident. I had been brought up somewhat sheltered from violence as a child. I was a church kid, the son of a church elder. Guns drawn, a beating, and blood was different and dangerous. However, the neighbourhood appeared to settle back into its routine. The Jamaican accents in Jamaica Plain in the heart of Boston, Massachusetts, and a mixture of soul and Caribbean melodies brushed away the insanity of that terrible moment.

I myself was able to relegate that scene to the back of my mind and instead focus on the great time I was having with my cousins in Boston that summer of 1972. There were also so many new experiences to take in. A man who approached me on Nantasket Beach marked my first encounter with a gay person. Scared and confused, I rebuffed his overtures and hurried away to rejoin my cousins. Boston was also where I first heard the plaintive strains of Bill Withers singing "Lean On Me." I listened to my cousins jamming in the basement of the campus of Northeastern University to which we had gained access through their friend Lance Forrester, a student there. Fritz was on guitar and also doing vocals; Paul on bass guitar, and Jerome on drums. We bought pizza at midnight, which was unheard of in the UK at the time. My cousins entered a talent contest at a television station. I found it weird being instructed when to applaud in order to embellish the program. I had my first McDonald's milkshake in Boston. The day was scorching hot. The milkshake was cool and crunchy from the ice particles coming through the thick straw. It was the best milkshake I had ever tasted.

We went to church on Saturdays at Berean Seventh-day Adventist Church. The humidity had my cousin's dress shirt clinging to his body, drenched with sweat even before we left the house to get to church. There were beautiful Black girls at the church who, I was surprised to learn, were only 16 to 18 years old; they looked like they were in their mid-20s. They certainly looked more mature than the 16 to 18-year-old girls in the UK. My wife would say they looked like they were "force riped." I engaged a few of them in light-hearted repartee and later learned that Lance, a handsome church member with a gorgeous Afro (a badge of honour in those days), was somewhat affronted that I had come encroaching on the territory of his female pursuits.

I also remember the special treat of my aunt's cooking. Her chicken, rice and peas, and other Jamaican dishes were always prepared with expert care. Aunt Claire was a loving and generous soul. When I left to return to the UK, she gave me a gift of money–so much so that I returned with more in my pocket than I had arrived with in America two months earlier.

I was having so much fun that before I knew it, there was a notice-able change from hot, humid temperatures to cool, fall-like breezes and it was time to return to England. My cousin Fritz had tried to interest me in applying to university in Massachusetts and a college in Alabama, which I took a hard look at because I knew my fortunes ultimately lay in getting a degree and a profession. But it wasn't to be. I was intimidated by the cost for a foreign student and the fact that all the grants dangled before me were exclusively for US citizens or residents. So, I dropped the idea. It would be back in England that I would have to search out the post-secondary education for which I could receive financial assis-tance, leading to a career that suited the strengths and personality I was still discovering within myself.

# PREPARING FOR A CAREER
## POST-SECONDARY EDUCATION

The very first thing I did literally one day after I returned from my trip to Boston was look for a college to attend in the UK. The details of how it happened are hazy in my mind but as I recall, I arrived back in England on a Friday or Saturday during the last week of August. On Sunday, I was reading the *Sunday Observer* newspaper and saw an advert for a Bachelor of Arts, Business Studies degree at South Bank Polytechnic in east central London. A few days later, at the beginning of September 1972, I was sitting in my first class after enrolling in record time. The advert was evidently intended to attract late applicants to fill remaining places because normally, applications for September of each year must be submitted by the preceding January or February.

There was nothing spectacular to me about that course. It was a four-year business studies degree program with one full year, the third year, spent on a work placement. I had thoughts of a career as a businessman, but I wasn't sure what that even meant. At the time, there was no specific occupation drawing me. The program was a grind I entered just to get a degree and see where it led.

Nonetheless, it was interesting to be in an educational cohort that included people other than predominantly White English people for the first time in my life. There was a Nigerian, an Indian woman called Laxmi Singh, I believe, an Asian woman, and an Egyptian called Fouad Rathle. I was closest to pipe-smoking Fouad, who I associated with exclusively at school and not socially. It was still a time in my life when socializing with people who didn't share my faith tradition was foreign to me. I was taken aback at his bold assertion that every country needed elites to govern the ignorant masses, but I loved his humour and good nature that manifested itself every time we parted when, in response to my "see you later," he'd reply without skipping a beat, "Not if I see you first."

During my college years, I lived in South London and rented rooms with Lawrence Sullivan, who was doing the same degree program as me. Time passed in a blur. One thing that stands out to me now was hearing another of the tenants, obviously profoundly disturbed, screaming in the middle of the night in what sounded like Polish or some other European language. I could only imagine what kind of trauma the man had experienced that shook him into terror-filled screaming during the early hours of each new day.

Another memory I have of that place was toward the end of my stay when I overheard another tenant, also a student, making out with his girlfriend. I assumed he was perhaps celebrating, with relief and obvious passion, the end of exams and the prospect of release from his tenancy. It was an activity that was anathema to me, having grown up with the injunction that sex before marriage was strictly forbidden and I would have to wait patiently until after my nuptials to experience it. Thanks to my naivety and judgmentalism, honed by years of church attendance, the two busy in the room next door were a case, as far as I was concerned, of "Father, forgive them for they know not what they do."

In my third year of the Business Studies degree program, I did my placement at Ford Motor Company's head office at Eagle Way, Warley, Essex. I worked on the fifth-floor pricing automotive parts and optional extras. Toward the end of my stint there, I show up each morning in good health, dressed smartly in a suit and tie. But every time I approached the doors to start my day's work, I'd develop a headache. I realized in later years that I was exhibiting one of the classic symptoms of burnout. I didn't understand what I was doing, I had no agency in the organization and frankly, pricing car parts left me cold.

In pursuit of an all-round business experience, I transferred to Human Resources after a few months and welcomed the different exposure to corporate life. I gained an insight into the movement of managers in the corporate system: no manager worth his (managers were mostly, if not exclusively, men back then) salt stayed in a management position for more than around two years. Many hopped from Ford to Chrysler and General Motors in their pursuit of more responsibilities and promotion to the higher echelons of the corporate automobile world. I heard the name of one of the executive stars of the automobile world, Lee Iacocca, for the first time, spoken with admiration and in hushed tones by aspiring Ford employees.

One of the mantras I kept hearing was that if you wanted to be a manager, you had to be ruthless. This went across the grain for me. I still had a lot to discover about myself, but I knew for certain that this was not who I was. In later years, I came to adopt an approach that melded a compassionate management style with firmness of action when dealing with the people I supervised. On a personal level, being treated with concern and empathy worked to get the best out of me. I had no problem with being guided with a firm hand. After all, I had been treated this way by my father, who applied his strictness with thoughtful and measured discipline, and I thank him for it. Experiencing him this way helped me to get back on track educationally and do my best to please him and my mother by applying myself with greater determination as I got older. When I became a manager myself later on in life, I brought a firm yet compassionate approach with me into the job. To me, ruthlessness was counterproductive and would not necessarily lead to better outcomes.

## CALL TO THE MINISTRY

It was in the third year of my business degree that I participated in a youth evangelistic campaign to attract people to join our church. We had meetings geared towards youth in the neighbourhood the church was in. The challenge we faced was to attracting young people from the predominantly White neighbourhood to our predominantly Black church. In an era that had just witnessed civil rights action in the United States, a time in which racism was being brought into sharp relief in my consciousness, it was bewildering yet not altogether surprising that we tended to attract other Black young people to our meetings. It was bewildering to me because we had faith in the power of our message and our earnest personalities. It was not surprising because it was evident then, and increasingly in later years, that the power of social stratification and disapproval of White people mixing with Black people was even stronger.

I enjoyed the work we did giving Bible studies. One young lady we were teaching our doctrines became increasingly drowsy and almost succumbed to sleep during a study of Daniel 8:14, a hallmark teaching of the Seventh-day Adventist Church. The study involved imbibing a denominationally packaged version of history and a tolerance for taking in copious amounts of information about dates and calculations of prophetic pronouncements, all designed to show how special our church was in the grand scheme of Earth's last days.

Notwithstanding, the fun I had in that campaign working with a young man, Costas Chrysaffis, a Greek Cypriot who came from the Wood Green Seventh-day Adventist Church, was part of what led to me deciding to become a minister. Perhaps more importantly, there was my personal conviction about the Christian message of love and caring for those around me. The Seventh-day Adventist message of a better life to come in the hereafter, with a banishing of the struggles of our current lives, was also appealing. I had witnessed first-hand how the Seventh-day Adventist Christian religion had supported my parents and helped them navigate life's pressing issues with a calm dignity. I wanted to share these messages.

I also recall one of the pastors of my home Holloway Seventh-day Adventist Church asking me years before whether I had considered going into the ministry. At the time, I dismissed the question quickly and almost flippantly by immediately replying "yes" to get him off my back so he wouldn't talk about it or try to browbeat me any further. But along with another person who had suggested the same thing, he planted a seed in my mind that stayed with me and eventually gained my acceptance. I later learned that like me, Costas had considered going into the ministry. But unlike me, he had decided against it and became an engineer instead.

I talked to Orville Woolford, a family friend, role model, and brilliant wise man, about my decision. His advice confirmed my sense that it would be prudent to finish my business studies degree first before enrolling for a theology degree. I finished my fourth year after pulling the only all-nighter I have ever experienced to complete an extended term paper or thesis about which I felt no real interest or passion.

It may seem that my whole time completing my degree at South Bank Polytechnic was a waste because I didn't pursue a career in business, but I learned valuable lessons about good business practices that stayed with me for the rest of my life. From that experience, I have concluded that no education is ever wasted and can be useful in whatever avenue of life in which one finds oneself. This lesson proved itself true many years later when I was minister of a church in Whitby, Ontario. With my understanding of depreciation and the importance of preparing for it, I had the church set aside funds for the replacement of deteriorating equipment in a separate account. It wasn't until after I had retired and left the church that I heard with satisfaction about how when the boiler broke down, the members were able, without stress on their finances, to install a new boiler with the funds set aside over the preceding years.

# A CHURCH IN CRISIS

During the four years I was pursuing my business studies degree (from 1972 to 1976), the real excitement had to do with events casting a dark shadow over the Seventh-day Adventist Church. Just prior to those four years, on June 26, 1971, our denomination had a Day of Fellowship or a national conference assembly that brought together more than 6,000 Seventh-day Adventist members from all over Britain.[6] It was held at the Royal Albert Hall and provided a prelude to a smaller gathering for a business session of the national church the following day at the Hemel Hempstead Pavilion. The Day of Fellowship was a big deal. The Royal Albert Hall gathering "was the largest in the history of the denomination in Britain."[7] The Saturday services involved Bible study presentations, singing of hymns, and musical performances as well as sermons to inspire and strengthen commitment to God and the Christian mission.

Renting that prestigious venue would have involved major long-range planning, including a well-thought-out budget. I was impressed by the greatness of the hall and the attendance of a committed membership who filled every seat. However, a remarkable realization began to emerge: the vast majority of the members sitting in the seats were Black. All of the members standing on the platform were White. There stood the British Union Conference president, the presidents of the local conferences, and various department directors and pastors–all were White. This did not escape the notice of the Black lay leaders in the audience that day.

6. Jack Mahon, "The Hope And The Glory," *British Advent Messenger* 76, no. 15, 16 (July 1971): 2.
7. Mahon, "The Hope And The Glory," 2.

I remember an agitated conversation taking place between those lay leaders at the end of the first service, which took place from about 9:00 a.m. until about 10:30 a.m. Three things were patently clear. Firstly, the Black membership was in the majority. Secondly, there were only a handful of Black ministers, and thirdly, the Black membership was not represented in the administration of the Church at the highest levels in Britain.

I heard the Black lay leaders, which included Orville Woolford, Lloyd Rennalls, Nylan Kennedy, Mike Kellawan, George Escoffery, Arthur Torrington, and my father Hymers Wilson, Sr., grumbling about the starkly overt omission. The symbolism carried with this omission was an in-your-face statement that White people were firmly in charge of the Church and we had no leaders to represent us. I heard that the lay leaders approached the Conference leadership to state their objections to what they were seeing. They demanded a Black presence on the platform for the next worship service, which was to take place at approximately 11:00 a.m. Realizing the obvious negative optics of a situation to which they appeared blithely ignorant of before, the Conference leadership scrambled. By the time the worship service started, Pastor Theodore McLeary, a Black pastor originally from Jamaica, was included in the platform party. The meeting proceeded as planned with that one significant change and worship unfolded without further incident.

It was an exciting and empowering moment for me as I watched my father and the other lay leaders not just grumble about the situation, but do something about it–making their demand for a seat at the table, as it were. I don't recall dad discussing the situation with me that day. I was eighteen years old at the time and that was something for grown-ups to talk about. In our home, at eighteen you didn't qualify to be in "big people's" conversations. I learned by watching just as I had learned to cook that quintessentially Jamaican dish, rice and peas, by watching my mother. A few years later when I was in my early twenties, dad cautioned me to choose my battles after I jumped up and made a public comment in a South England Conference (SEC) constituency meeting. But discussions about strategy were something he did with his contemporaries in the Laymen's Forum while I looked on and listened.

So, I watched and learned and was proud to see that we, our people, Black people, had a voice. We had agency. The importance of that moment at the Royal Albert Hall in June 1971 stayed with me for the rest of my life. It certainly was a prelude to the events that followed in the Church, especially over the next four years and beyond.

## A SEISMIC SHIFT

That Day of Fellowship marked the beginning of a seismic shift in the Seventh-day Adventist Church in the UK. Black lay leaders became bolder in demanding change. They seized on the idea of forming a laymen's forum, loosely affiliating themselves with the Association of Adventist Forums that had been formed in the United States in the 1960s (principally, but not exclusively, to facilitate communication on academic ideas and opinions among Adventist scholars). The Black lay leaders formed the London Laymen's Forum (LLF) and produced a magazine called *Comment* that they used to promote their message

Photo of some of the members of the London Laymen's Forum who agitated for black representation in the leadership of the South England Conference of the Seventh-day Adventist Church. Pictured from left to right: Hymers Wilson Sr., Orville Woolford, Martin Rodney, Nylan Kennedy, Lloyd Rennalls.

to the church membership, urging acceptance of the idea of greater Black representation in administrative leadership.

Every week that went by from that time on saw some new development. Arthur Torrington wrote an article called "The Goose that Laid the Golden Egg." It was named after the famous story in *Aesop's Fables* that teaches how greed can lead to great loss and highlights moral values such as honesty and truth. Circulated widely to the Adventist membership in London, Torrington's paper argued that the SEC administration was happy to accept the money donated by Black church members in tithes and offerings, but unwilling to grant them any say at higher levels of leadership. The Black membership was, in effect, the goose laying the golden egg.

The figures Torrington extrapolated from a rough estimate of the membership of the SEC made this clear. At the same time, he argued that the SEC leadership was not as accepting of the idea of the participation of Black people in conference leadership. The SEC leadership got wind of the document. The administration was clearly incensed by the accusation and swiftly requested the Holloway Seventh-day Adventist Church to remove Arthur Torrington or Torry, the name we called him, from membership by disfellowshipping him.

I was on the Holloway Church board in my capacity as youth leader for that local church when it considered this request. I remember our mood; board members saw the SEC request as an affront. The membership of the board was almost all Black. We all knew that Torry's article painted an accurate picture of the situation. We knew we were ardent financial contributors to the local church and the higher organization. We donated tithes and offerings to the cause.

According to denominational rules stated in its church manual, tithes (a tenth of one's income) went into the coffers of the umbrella organization. Local churches were not allowed to retain a penny of that money. Amounts considered "free-will offerings" were sums of money church members donated over and above the tithe donations, and it was this money that could be retained by the local church. Most Adventists are more particular about donating tithes than freewill offerings. As a result, many churches in the Seventh-day Adventist denomination are strapped for cash to fund their local mission while the umbrella organizations are replete with money for department heads and their budgets, including travel budgets that enable trips to international meetings. Ironically, local churches find themselves in the unenviable position of having to plead with the higher organization, namely the area conference, for funds to help with community outreach or church-building projects.

We knew that Black members were in the majority and our donations were keeping the SEC finances in the black, so to speak. We knew, as well, that it was patently obvious there were no Black administrators. At the time, there were only about three Black ministers: ordained pastor Theodore McLeary, and two not-yet-ordained pastoral interns, Clifford Pitt and Rudy Bailey.

There was no way we were going to throw Torry under the bus. We were well aware that the SEC had limits on their authority, and they could only pressure the local church into sanctioning him. The motion was probably brought to the Church board by our pastor, the only conference employee on the Church board, or by the White elder Marcel Guenin. At any rate, we were not going to yield to the pressure and when the vote was taken to approve his disfellowshipping, the motion failed by a significant majority. The LLF saw it as a huge victory. It signalled that Black members could not be pushed around by the Conference. I personally felt a sense of pride in our people. We had agency. We were doing our part in the wake of the Civil Rights protests in the United States. This was our small contribution to standing up and defending our right to be heard, acknowledged, and represented in leadership at the highest levels of the church.

In South England, the SEC leadership saw the LLF as a threat. The forum wasn't properly established through recognized church channels, so they sought to ban it and steer members away from it. Undeterred, the LLF pressed on, holding meetings with Black elders across London. I remember meetings held in Brixton at Ferndale Road, the site of the local SDA church, with Brixton, Lewisham, and Balham church elders and officers. In subsequent meetings, they were joined by elders from Tottenham and a few other churches. The LLF went even further afield, meeting in North British Conference territory with elders in Handsworth, Birmingham. I remember a meeting held in the home of the Stewart clan with Oscar, Ashmore, and Frankie Stewart as the main participants.

The SEC began to realize that the LLF was a serious movement and on April 4, 1974, voted in action 73 to "formulate the basis for the establishment of a local Conference Advisory Committee in South England." It was proposed that at a future Committee meeting, "further discussion could be given to this matter in order to meet the needs and concern expressed by some of the London Elders." Some of those so-called London Elders were, in fact, LLF members concerned about the lack of Black representation in higher leadership positions. Their proposal was no doubt a response to invitations from the LLF to the SEC to talk about the issues faced by the Black membership.

By October, action still had not been taken to form this Conference Advisory Committee, and the LLF perceived the process as moving along like molasses flowing uphill. What the SEC did do was set up the Conference Lay Advisory Council, saying it was to improve communication between the SEC and the churches. They then appointed the SEC president as Chairman of the Conference Lay Advisory Council. This was regarded by the lay leadership who formed the LLF as an attempt by the SEC to control the agenda and tamp down what they appeared to regard as rebellion. Strategically, LLF leaders had found their way onto the Conference Lay Advisory Council and now had two fronts on which to make their concerns heard: the LLF *and* the Lay Advisory Council.

By Christmas 1974, Orville Woolford, a close family friend who became the Trans European Division of Seventh-day Adventist Education Director in the 1990s, wrote in *Comment* that "[t]he London Laymen's Forum ... with diligence and dispatch collected the problems, prayerfully prepared suggestions for solving them, and attempted to submit all to the local conference administrators. Alas they refused to listen. The submission was then made to the General Conference administrators whose further action we still await."[8]

To strengthen their protest about the situation in the Conference, three London churches withheld sending tithes to the SEC. This major departure from procedure very quickly came to the attention of the General Conference administration in Washington, DC, which functioned as a headquarters of the worldwide Seventh-day Adventist Church. There was no doubt that it posed a significant threat to the functioning of the Church in South England and regions beyond. What if other churches did the same thing? If the action went unchecked, it was argued that the money to employ pastors, church school teachers, and administrators would quickly dry up and seriously stymie the work of the church in the UK.

---

8. Orville Woolford, *Comment* 1, no. 4 (November/December 1974).

In addition, there was the further threat of a split to form Black and White conferences in the UK, specifically in the territory comprising the SEC, which again could spread to other parts of Britain. In an action under the heading "Integration and Growth," the SEC Executive Committee voted on February 3, 1976 for the British Union Conference to create a subcommittee tasked with determining the feasibility of establishing a Regional Conference.[9] We were familiar with what this meant because there were in the denomination, particularly in the United States, regional conferences that had Black leadership and predominantly Black memberships in the churches under the umbrella of those conferences. Regional conferences operated in the same geographical areas as White conferences that had jurisdiction over predominantly White congregations. It was a kind of apartheid or "separate but equal" arrangement.

The January 1977 issue of *Comment* reveals an interesting background to that SEC Executive Committee action. It came out of a recommendation formulated by a Plans (planning) Committee at the 50th SEC Session at Plymouth in May 1975. The recommendation that sparked the SEC action proposed ways of promoting greater integration and specifically asked for "fuller black representation at all levels of the work."

The author of the January 1977 *Comment* article stated,

> 'The South England Conference Executive Committee' ... nominated a sub-committee to consider this recommendation on 'Integration' ... Pastor McLeary puts it succinctly in an article that was refused publication by the

---

9. SEC Executive Committee Minutes, 3 February 1976, Action 10, Subsection 3.

British Advent Messenger (its title "The reasons which necessitated the study of the feasibility of Regional Conference"). The sub-committee met and after a while it became clear that black representation at departmental level was unacceptable to the Conference Leaders.

[Pastor McCleary] continued, 'It was then proposed that a London Conference might be the answer, but this was also unacceptable.' He went on to show that it was from these deliberations that 'the idea of a Regional Conference was born.'

There were two Blacks on the committee, neither of whom were responsible for the proposal for Regional Conference.[10]

Pastor McCleary's article was refused publication in the British Union Conference of Seventh-day Adventist's magazine precisely because it exposed the embarrassing fact that no Black member had asked for a separation of Black from White administrations. Instead, it was the White members of the SEC Executive Committee who had pushed the idea.

The implications of what Pastor McLeary was documenting were clear to us all. Everybody at the time knew what that meant. Black people wanted to be represented in an integrated conference leadership, but this was being rejected. Regional conferences had come into existence as a result of the failure of the White-controlled Adventist Church system in United States to allow for the development and advancement of Black leadership. The tipping point came when a Black woman was refused treatment in a Seventh-day Adventist hospital and died due to a protracted stay in its drafty hallways. The reaction of utter dismay of Black leaders and members at this incident was said to have contributed significantly to the establishment of Regional Conferences in the United States.

---

10. G.S. Escoffery, "Which Way Now," *Comment 4*, no.1, (January 1977): 4.

If the British Union Conference of Seventh-day Adventists found that a regional conference would be feasible, it would have meant yet another failure in yet another country to allow for the presence, development, and advancement of Black leadership. In the SEC in Britain, the split between Black and White would become an overt reality.

The urgency of the situation, undoubtedly heightened by the potential loss of tithe income, led to a meeting organized for dialogue between the LLF, the British Union Conference and its member conferences, and the General Conference leadership. The latter included Robert H. Pierson, the General Conference president who came to the United Kingdom from the church's headquarters in Maryland in the United States. My father, Hymers Wilson Sr., was one of the LLF representatives. Orville Woolford was another, along with Nylan Kennedy, George Escoffery, Lloyd Rennalls, Mike Kellawan, and Martin Rodney, as far as I can remember.

The dialogue produced a document titled the *Consultative Document British Union Conference of Seventh-day Adventists 1978*. It was known informally as "the Pierson Package." A statement from page one reads "we prefer the above approach of racial integration to racial segregation through separate Conference organizations. Christ himself recognized no distinction of nationality or race. He came to break down every wall of partition and separation. The divine injunction still is 'All ye are brethren' (Matthew 28:8)."[11]

---

11. *Consultative Document British Union Conference of Seventh-day Adventists 1978* (British Union Conference, 1978): 1.

Agreed to by all parties, the Pierson Package effectively killed any move toward having Black conferences in Britain. It meant that instead of regional (Black) conferences, there was an understanding laid out in the document that would determine a multi-racial mix of administrators and department leaders at the conference level. This included the hiring of Black pastors to bring their numbers up to reasonable levels in order to oversee those churches with predominantly Black memberships. One could argue that this action was consistent with the lofty ideals of integration and giving everyone a seat at the administrative table. Yet I remember thinking (as did others in our group) that if the decision had gone the other way and if our desire to be represented in leadership had been spurned, we would have made a regional conference in England work. After all, we had heard reports of the successful development of their Black leaders and the explosive growth of the Black churches they led in the United States.

My view of the Church I had grown up in, participating in its mission of mutually nurturing its members, helping the needy in the community, and engaging in outreach that attempted to attract new members, was never the same again after those years in the early 1970s. I now saw a side of the functioning of the Seventh-day Adventist Church that was political and appeared at times, in its machinations, at odds with the ideals of Jesus and the Golden Rule (namely, loving others as one loves oneself). A new reality presented itself to me: that being a church member and claiming to be a Christian did not necessarily mean a person was cured of the curse of racism. The Church as an institution did not necessarily act in ways that were right and just for their own sake, but often only acted in response to pressure and agitation. Black members who came to Britain expecting full partnership in the Church instead had to fight for seats in leadership. They did so by first learning the rules and regulations of the church, then using political process to achieve their own objectives.

For me, this was profoundly enlightening. I saw how Black members, including my own father, were skilful at seeing the ecclesiastical landscape for what it was–how they adapted and organized themselves into an efficient group and assumed an unofficial but effective role in advocating for the wider Black Seventh-day Adventist community. If they could do it, I could do it, too. Back in those days, the word "politics" was a dirty one in the Church. After all, the Church was supposed to function as the hands and feet of Jesus. Through my experiences watching the "struggle," as I call it, of the Church in the 1970s, I learned that politics is the art and science of government. I witnessed how vital it is to be aware of this very fact in order to achieve one's rights.

This meant I had to reorient my personal spiritual experience. I was no longer as loyal to the Church as an institution. In contrast, my primary loyalty to God was now stronger. I could see things I viewed in the institutionalized Church critically and challenge them as the Church was no longer perfect in my eyes. Instead, it was made up of human beings who had their faults and I had a responsibility, as did any other member, to evaluate the actions of the institution and call for accountability in harmony with the teachings of Jesus that it espoused.

## NEWBOLD COLLEGE YEARS

From late summer and early fall 1976 to just before Christmas 1979,

I attended the Adventist-owned Newbold College in Berkshire, UK. I was training to become one of those Black pastors envisioned in the Pierson Package. The early influx came in from the east and west Caribbean and the United States to fill the need as a matter of urgency. I was going to be among the first of the homegrown Black pastors, preceded by men such as Errol Lawrence, Hugo Kennedy, Cliff Pitt, Rudy Bailey, Vince Goddard, and Audley Charles, who had graduated from Newbold College and Andrews University's Theological Seminary in Berrien Springs, Michigan, a few years before I did with my Master of Divinity degree. Other Black theology students who arrived at the same time as me included Theo Stewart, Jeff Brown, Volney Ham-Ying, and Humphrey Walters, to name a few.

I had a fantastic time at Newbold College. The male and female friends I met there I still have contact with to this day, over 40 years later, thanks to Facebook. The college boasted an enrollment from about 40 different countries. It was a time of meeting North and South Americans, Scandinavians, Nordics, and Europeans from the east and west as well as students from the Middle East, Africa, and Australasia. I developed relationships with some beautiful young women there–some closer than others, such as Americans Judy Reisz (now Judy Reisz Bedell), Renée Hill, Robin Duska (now Robin Duska Huff), and Aðalheiður Birgisdottir from Iceland. Having attended an all-boys grammar school, developing these types of friendships was a first for me.

It was fun mastering Greek, or at least mastering New Testament Greek as taught by Pastor John 'Daddy' Dunnett, a quintessential

Englishman with an eccentric delivery and scrupulous attention to detail. From him and other professors at Newbold College I learned an almost fanatical punctuality that reinforced my father's own brand, perhaps from his stint in the military during World War II.

Even here though, with the serene setting of the Berkshire countryside providing the backdrop for those halcyon college days, the shadow of racism was never completely out of sight and out of mind. Noticing a group of West Indians sitting together, laughing and having fun with our usual exuberance in the cafeteria, the men's preceptor, Pastor Alan Crowe, approached us one day with a complaint. "Why do you always sit together? You should mix with the others."

This was an affront to me and my West Indian fellow students on a number of counts. We were always mixing with the other nationalities and had great relationships with them. There was a residence requirement at the college, which meant that all students lived on the college campus (with the exception of some married students who lived nearby in the Binfield, Berkshire community). Almost every Saturday night, we sat in the dormitory lounge with students of all nationalities and watched Match of the Day on television, which featured a full-length soccer game held earlier that day. Black students participated in the various clubs on campus. I was appointed parliamentarian of the Newbold Students' Association during my very first year at Newbold. I was the only Black person on the Association's board. I was the editor of *Prism*, the college's student newspaper. I sang in a group that travelled to various churches in South England with the goal of promoting the college. I sang with only two other Black students, Theo Stewart (who was British) and Tom

Prasado-Rao (an East Indian-American), as well as Kay Campbell (American), Chris Harle (an Englishman), and Beverley Emm (Canadian). I had White girlfriends at Newbold, as well. I was also one of a handful of Black students in the college choir that sang on Saturdays for the main church services.

As far as I am aware, Alan Crowe never approached any of the other nationalities with the same complaint—even though the Finnish men tended to cluster together, the Norwegians did the same, and other nationalities tended to sit in their groups due to their common background and shared experiences. There was no animosity with the other nationalities, no rivalry apart from the five-a-side soccer games in the gym where the national groups of students tended to form into teams. To put this all into perspective, of the approximately 250 Newbold students, there were only about twenty Black students in total! Pastor Crowe's complaint was unfounded on so many levels, given how fully integrated I and my friends sitting at that cafeteria table were in the life and functioning of the college.

For me, the highlight of the five-a-side soccer games mentioned above was an epic final match between the West Indians and the Icelandic teams. The Icelandic men were fantastic players with some deadly scorers. When we West Indians, who most Newbold students felt were the favourites to win, realized we were going to play them in a final match, I knew we were in for a tough battle. I decided to strategically downplay our abilities. I began to tell everybody I met that the Icelanders had a great team and we'd have a hard time beating them. As I look back on that strategy, I know that no professional team I've seen talking about their expectations for the outcome ever goes into a game using a strategy like that. Certainty of a win is a vital mental part of pre-game build up. Anyway, knowing we had deadly scorers of our own and a classy team, I reasoned that I needed to inject a false sense of security into the minds of both the Iceland team, their supporters, and others who would be spectators.

The game lived up to its hype: the Iceland team played extremely well. They attacked and defended, then scored with precision and efficiency. We held as best we could, but it was tough going. With minutes to go to full time, they were actually ahead by 2-1. Now, it was a matter of pride. Although we were West Indians, we were also Brits and in those days, there was no such thing as an Icelandic team that rated anywhere of significance internationally. We would never be able to live down the shame of being beaten by a team from Iceland. Somehow, we levelled the game and went on to score the winning goal with a shot by Jeff Brown from a seemingly impossible angle. Our reputation and pride were intact.

Alas, as my time at Newbold quickly drew to an end, I began to feel jaded. I was in the Master of Divinity (MDiv) program, an Andrews University program one could start at Newbold in the UK and complete at Andrews University in the United States. This MDiv program ran on the ten-week quarter system. The majority of the other students at Newbold, who were doing bachelor's degrees or taking English-language classes, were on the semester system. This meant that when I arrived for my fifth quarter at Newbold in September 1979, it was already weeks after the other students who had arrived in August. They had already met each other and formed relationships, which happens at warp speed with young adults in their late teens and early 20s. I didn't fit into any group very easily. Most of the students I had known and were close to the previous school year had left. Now age 26 and older than most of the other students, I felt like a fish out of water.

By Christmas 1979, I left Newbold after completing five quarters. According to then-President of the College Dr. Jan Paulsen, no doubt fuelled by his desire to maintain the enrollment levels at Newbold College, it was mandatory to complete at least six 10-week quarters at Newbold before moving onto Andrews University. Instead, I followed the advice of Terry Joshua, the former Newbold Student Association president who himself had already left Newbold for Andrews University to complete his MDiv. Terry made it clear that I could leave Newbold College any time I wanted to. All I needed to show to Andrews University was my academic transcripts outlining what I had accomplished at Newbold College, and this would be credited toward completion of my MDiv.

The Newbold College years were a significant time of personal growth for me. I was forging my own path in life. I looked to my peers for guidance especially in academic areas, but also for ways to earn money to pay for my college tuition and residence fees. During summer breaks and through the student grapevine, I found out about and got jobs in Norway and Canada. I was learning how to fend for myself, developing the resilience to navigate life and avoid being overshadowed by prejudice whenever it emerged in its subtle or overt forms. I was learning to balance the fun I was having for the bulk of the time I was at Newbold with studying diligently so I could progress to the next level and become a pastor.

No longer was I the class clown. Those days were long gone and I adopted a totally new approach to my life as a student. After all, there was a lot more at stake: I didn't have any expectations of going back home and being supported financially by my parents. During my three years and three months as a student at Newbold, the longest period I spent back home between college and summer jobs was three weeks! I knew I now had to make my own way in life and I was determined to do just that.

## A STARK REVELATION

Prior to my final term at Newbold, during the summer of 1979, I had worked in British Columbia (BC), Canada, to earn my school fees for both Newbold College and Andrews University. I had gotten the job through a fellow student named Diana Curtis (now Diana Grønning), an Aboriginal woman who knew Steve Crombie, who ran a logging operation in BC. The first time he set eyes on me he said, "I didn't realize you had a suntan." I was paid the princely sum of $7.00 Canadian per hour. It was a lot at that time, even though I received the lowest pay on the logging site. I had the experience of my life working as a skidder driver, setting my own chokers made of metal cables around hemlocks and spruce and other tree logs whose names escape me, and dragging them out of the bush down to the seashore where they would be prepared to float away on the water to where they would be sold.

Because Steve knew I was training to be a minister, he engineered a preaching appointment for me in Vernon, BC. After the sermon, I was invited to the home of a German man and his wife for lunch. He took me for a drive through the BC countryside. Pointing out vast tracts of land he said belonged to the Aboriginals, he nonchalantly explained that they didn't work hard like the White man. That remark overshadowed the hospitality of the man and his wife. Never one to react quickly to slights, I reflected on his remark sometime later and the full force of his insensitivity and racism exploded in my brain.

There I was, a young Black man, listening to a German man explaining the virtue of White industry in contrast to his view of the lack of effort on the part of the non-White "Indians." It was clear he didn't really "see" me. I wasn't White, but it didn't occur to him that I might take offence. Years later, as I began to fully embrace the knowledge of the industry of my Black ancestors on whose backs the White British, Europeans, Americans, Australians, and South Africans became immensely wealthy, it intensified in my mind the ignorance of that man's blithe remark. He had expressed a false conception of the superiority of White people that was cemented into his mind.

I recall walking one day in central London near Westminster Abbey, the Houses of Parliament, and other bastions of British enterprise and thinking about how they were built. I noticed the distinctively Georgian architecture characterized by its proportion and balance. The construction of its most direct and famous example, Buckingham Palace, began in 1831 and was commissioned by King George III for his wife, Queen Charlotte. I started to piece together a narrative in my own mind. Emerging with a growing clarity was an awareness that the buildings I was gazing upon had been financed by proceeds of the Triangular Trade that brought immense wealth to British shores.

The Trade involved European ships bringing manufactured goods, weapons, and liquor in exchange for slaves on the first leg of the three-part journey. The second part involved transporting African men, women, and children to the Americas to serve as slaves. On the third leg, they exported raw materials from the colonies to Europe.[12] I reasoned that the manifestations of opulent wealth in the buildings in front of me were, in fact, created on the backs of my ancestors toiling until they were literally worked to death in the hot sun. I concluded that I had a stake in this wealth. I belonged because of the work of my forebears. This belonged as much to them, meaning my Black ancestors, as it did to the plantation owners and their progeny benefitting in the present from that legacy.

Then, a thought struck me: I was English, not an immigrant. I was born in Jamaica, but I had a right to be here–a right earned by the blood and sweat of my African ancestors. It was a quiet, private reflection, yet one that made me see myself differently in English society. I was not even just British, but specifically English. This was a subtle designation I took on in my earlier years but I found that I could hold my head even higher. It made me stronger. My self-esteem was fortified even more than before.

## SEMINARY TRAINING

With my earnings from logging in BC supplemented by a grant from the British Union Conference of Seventh-day Adventists, I enrolled at Andrews University's Theological Seminary in Berrien Springs, Mich-

---

12. "Ch. 16-3 & 24-2 Guided Reading," Auburn.wednet.edu, https://www.auburn.wednet.edu/cms/lib03/WA01001938/Centricity/Domain/2351/TP%205%20Weekly%20Packet.docx

igan. My time at Andrews University completing my MDiv was my third visit in the United States. This time, I was there for a year and four months, from March 1980 until a day or two after the royal wedding of Charles and Diana in July 1981.

In contrast to Newbold College, Andrews University was spacious. There were beautifully manicured grounds verdant with a variety of trees and bushes. There were tennis courts and many buildings housing classrooms, administrative offices, the seminary, a library, a centre where students could practice musical instruments and borrow music materials, and the huge centrepiece: the Pioneer Memorial Church (PMC). There were also student accommodations with separate build-ings for men and women as well as for married students and their families. The food was plentiful. Whereas we only received a single helping of salad in a small side dish with our meal in the Newbold cafeteria, we could take as much salad as we wanted at the Andrews cafeteria. The same was true for all the food. We could take as much as we could put on our plates. They even had a host in the Andrews cafeteria, a gracious middle-aged woman with immaculately coiffed, dyed hair who exuded charm and warmth, welcoming us and inviting us to enjoy our meal.

This belied the shadow that hung over the cafeteria experience. On one side of the cafeteria sat the White students with a few Black students sprinkled among them. On the other side were the Black students. I remember a food fight breaking out one afternoon between two groups of White students. They were whooping and hollering as each side sought to accurately pelt the other with the contents of their dishes. We Black students looked on with disdain and disbelief. Throwing food at somebody was foreign to me and, I suspect, to the West Indian and African Americans sitting around me. Greg Allen, who was from New York, stood up in disgust and shouted at the White students to quit their foolishness. The food fight ended as quickly as it began—not because of Greg's stern expressions of disgust, but because it petered out naturally as the students got out of their systems the thrill and excitement of launching their unwanted alimentary items toward their rivals. I heard nothing further about it. No announcements to discourage its reoccurrence. No apparent consequences for the perpetrators.

I learned that the division of who sat where in the cafeteria was a symptom of a wider rift between Blacks and Whites in America. This rift ran deeper than I had picked up in my previous two trips to the United States. Black students I met wouldn't even play country music. It was White 'hee-haw' music as far as they were concerned (ironically, as I have come to realize that some of the greatest country western singers are Black).

I had my own experience of trying to cross the lines of division in the cafeteria that a few Black students seemed to have successfully broken through. It happened when I saw, on the White side of the cafeteria, Judy Reisz, a fellow student I recognized from my time at Newbold in the UK. She and I had been close at Newbold, where we had first met when I saw her sitting on a wall near the cafeteria looking sad and dejected. I went up to her and she confided in me that she was homesick and missing her folks in America. I did what I could to cheer her up and we became great friends. We were on the student association board together at Newbold when Terry Joshua was president and I was the parliamentarian. Judy had this frog character we had fun with. We called each other Wide Mouth Frog (WMF). We had this beautiful platonic relationship and she had a lovely friendly spirit. To this day on Facebook, we exchange our greetings and call each other WMF (sometimes using an image of a green frog with a wide mouth), which must be bewildering to our other Facebook friends.

Now a few years later in 1980, when I recognized Judy sitting there, I went over from the so-called Black side to where she was sitting. To my recollection, the encounter was somewhat strained. Perhaps the passage of the three years since seeing her at Newbold had something to do with it or it could have been that she was sitting with her boyfriend John, who she later married, and with all the other White students around her. I was out of my comfort zone. I said my "hello, it's been a long time since I last saw you, how have you been?" There was a bit more small talk and then I retreated into the relative comfort of the 'Black' side of the cafeteria. The Andrews cafeteria wasn't at all like Newbold's, where people of all nationalities sat and ate together with no overtly cemented racial divisions. As I compared the two places in my mind, I missed the relatively relaxed Newbold environment. But from my reading of America's history of slavery, lynchings, and quest for civil rights, I understood very clearly the dynamics playing out before me.

Those dynamics also explain why we had Black Students Christian Fellowship (BSCF) and the Black Students Association of the Seminary (BSAS). Friday nights would feature special Black speakers and music from Black gospel singers, such as Lorraine Stewart (née McPherson) and Chloe Logan, who sang "Naaman the Leper" and brought us to our feet with rousing applause as she extolled in her powerful voice the power of God to heal. We heard stories of celebrated Black preachers such as Earl E. Cleveland, a charismatic evangelist who spoke his mind on Black issues, being refused permission to preach in PMC, the main church at Andrews University. It was that shadow thing again.

With its unofficial voluntary segregation, the Andrews experience was foreign to me. But the system I encountered at Andrews nudged me into acquiescence or else endure the scorn of my Black friends. Nor was I nudged unwillingly or unwittingly–I found solace there as I, a West Indian who grew up in the UK, shared common experiences with the African Americans and West Indians who had grown up in the Caribbean, the United States, and Canada. I remember swapping stories with African Americans about beatings received at the hands of our parents. We had this in common and we joked about our experiences, which we believed set us apart from the Whites. I personally was never brutalized by my father or mother, but I did receive my fair share of licks. I was, however, well familiar with stories from my own community of West Indians living in England. There was one in particular of a teenage boy who had committed some misdeed and received indescribable brutal beatings with a belt that left welts on the back from his God-fearing Christian father, a stalwart in the church I attended as a boy.

Some of the African Americans I met at Andrews were veterans of the Vietnam War. I remember one time walking down a row of the J. N. Andrews library and turning the corner to go down another, and startling one of those veterans. He immediately and automatically went into a defensive 'at the ready to fight' position but relaxed when, I imagine, he realized he was in the library in Berrien Springs, Michigan, with no threat of coming face-to-face with a 'brother.'

During my time at Andrews, I had brief relationships with several young women. One was Jenny Brown, who went on to make a name for herself as a musician and music educator. Another was Jackie Henry, who had an amazing singing voice. Other seminarians egged me on to get to know Regina Walker. I approached her in the Andrews library one day and, mustering all my courage, introduced myself. I was from England studying theology at the seminary and so on. When I finished my little speech, she looked me dead in the eyes and said, "Well, who are you anyway?" I was unprepared for the directness of the question. Somehow, I maintained my composure and eventually managed to have at least one date with her. It was soon clear she wasn't as enamoured with me as I was with her, and that relationship became stillborn.

There was also Cheryl Easley, a brilliant woman who already had her PhD and lived with her mother close to Andrews University. I experienced my first sauna, which was in the basement of Cheryl and her mother's house. We enjoyed great moments together, including an afternoon trip to Warren Dunes and a trip to meet her friends and extended family in Cincinnati, Ohio. It was there that I attended my very first baseball game. I hardly understood what was going on, having no knowledge of the intricacies of the game, but the sun was warm and it was a learning experience to take in that most American of games.

The highlight of my time at Andrews University was meeting Joy Benjamin. I first met Joy in the student centre with her friends, a group of about four or five of them altogether. I didn't pay much attention to her at first, but the next time I saw her was when I was looking for a date to take to a banquet organized by church officials from the West Indies Union of Seventh-day Adventists. They had invited any students to this banquet who were from the Caribbean, whether they lived in the Caribbean or not. I was at the entrance to the girls' dormitory's Lamson Hall chapel with my buddy Theo Stewart wondering who to take to the banquet when out of the chapel came Joy. Never one to hesitate, I immediately asked her to come to the banquet with me. She blinked her eyes a few times from the sheer blindsiding surprise of my approach, but agreed. It was a revealing testament to her spirit of adventure and spontaneity. We had a great time at the banquet and after the briefest of hiccups, I proposed to her within two and a half months of that first date. She said "yes" once again.

My immediate family, some cousins, aunts, and uncles, all met my fiancée Joy for the first time at my graduation ceremony when I received my Master of Divinity degree at Andrews University. Joy ironed my graduation gown in preparation for the ceremonies. It was a small act, nothing major in the grand scheme of things, but it was an act of caring and attentiveness that impressed me. I knew that having resolved to marry her, I was on the right track even though I had proposed to her after only dating for such a very short time. We've been married now for 42 years and have never looked back.

# GETTING ESTABLISHED
## BACK IN THE UK

It would be about another year and a half from the time I graduated from Andrews University to the time Joy and I got married. She stayed in the United States to finish her studies, and I returned to the UK. It was a time for me to focus on settling down, making enough money for accommodation, food, and transportation. At first, starting in August 1981, I worked for the Adventist Church at their new John Loughborough Secondary School as its bursar or business manager. On the pay I received, I couldn't afford to pay market-value rent. That was a reality check for me because I had every expectation when I was at university that armed with my Master of Divinity degree, I'd be able to get a decent pastoral job and afford rent.

I remember being at Andrews University in America and seeing former students pulling up in their nice cars (no doubt some of them rentals) dressed to impress, ready to participate in homecoming events on campus. They carried an air of confidence and self-assurance. They happily greeted their former classmates with tight, lingering hugs, many rocking back and forth with the sheer exuberance of their reunions. There was an unspoken understanding that each one had made it in the working world. They looked happy and satisfied. Alas, in contrast, I had to swallow expectations of a similar experience along with my pride and live with my parents in Wood Green, London, again.

My fortunes changed when, in March 1982, I became employed as a pastor. I interned first under Pastor Cecil Perry, then under Dr. Vassel Kerr. After going from working at a Seventh-day Adventist school to a church, my salary increase allowed me to rent a flat in Anerley Park in southeast London. Church officials used to dance around the subject of pay for teachers and other denominational school staff compared to the pay for ministers. I experienced a big boost to my income when I transitioned to being a minister. Imagine my surprise when, at a presentation to teachers, SEC official Martin Anthony asserted that the salaries of both teachers and pastors were the same. He may have been technically correct; however, what he failed to also add was that ministers received book and rent allowances and a few other financial perks that pushed their incomes up to levels where they could just about afford to make ends meet. By contrast, three or four young teachers I knew at the SEC's John Loughborough School had to pool their meagre resources to afford to pay rent and live in a house owned by the Conference.

By December 1982, my status changed again. I travelled from England to get married in Ottawa, Canada, Joy's home after immigrating years before as a teenager from Grenada in the West Indies. I was dressed appropriately for transatlantic jet travel in those days, in a smart suit and tie. Joy and I had a brief but memorable honeymoon in Bermuda and afterward, I flew back with my new bride to England. Our first marital home was in Norbury in South London. We then moved to North London and a new pastorate in Stoke Newington and Tottenham. This was my first introduction to shadowy rental practices.

I remember going to the offices of one of the rental property managers. Joy and I sat across from a very polite property manager who wanted to know what we were looking for. We wanted to rent a house. We were looking for accommodation befitting my station in life as a newly minted pastoral intern, a home in which we could feel comfortable.

In those days, everything was on paper. There were no computers or e-mail or search engines. The nearest thing to Google was the googly that spin bowlers in the game of cricket would cunningly bowl to an opposing batsman to get him out. Everything was written by hand in a thick book with line upon line of available rental properties. The property manager referred to the copious notes in front of him, scanning the instructions to see if there was a fit between what we wanted and what the owners were offering. I glimpsed the upside down writing across from me and realized that some of the notes clearly stated, "No non-Europeans."

Call me slow, but the fact that we were able to eventually find a house to rent in a fairly nice area erased that quiet snub from my mind. Perhaps it was because it was a tad gentler than the "no dogs, no Blacks, no Irish" written boldly on signs on the front doors of houses in previous years. Or maybe it was because it merely registered as the way things were and besides, we eventually found ourselves in Roundhill Drive in Enfield, Middlesex, on a quiet leafy residential street–a picture of English tranquility.

As I look back, I shudder at the banality of the racism we encountered. It was so ho-hum. It escaped our focus and the lack of attention we paid I can only put down to our homing in on other priorities, such as working diligently with what we could get and dwelling on maintaining a positive and cheerful home for ourselves and the children who were to come. I believe that approach was part of an instinctive survival strategy–keep our heads down and carry on regardless–because the alternative may have been to go completely bonkers under the weight of the realization that we weren't wanted in certain places. There was a shadow. I saw it. I noticed it. But in a moment, it was gone. I see value in that approach; it doesn't help to dwell on the slights one experiences. To live in that space is soul-destroying. I couldn't have pressed on with my life if I did and, to be frank, I don't think anybody who encounters rejection and slights can make it through life ruminating constantly about experiences of being nudged aside.

The years between 1982 and 1986 were consumed with getting established in my chosen career. Pastor. Minister of Religion for official documents, such as passports, bank loans and for any organization that needed to know my occupation. The title carried a certain amount of prestige. Initially, I had been working to prove I was worthy of moving up from intern to ordained pastor. This transition meant I would move to a higher level of respect and gain a few more points on the percentage scale, as far as salary was concerned. In the British context for our denomination, a three-year waiting period within which this promotion would happen was a reasonable expectation. Other denominations ordain their ministers immediately after graduating with their divinity degrees. Years later, as a youth director of the Church in South

England, I visited Pakistan and Zimbabwe. In those countries in the late 1980s and early 1990s, I learned that it wasn't uncommon for the missionaries to hold off on ordaining ministers for up to 10 years. In North America, a Union Conference official recently inexplicably held up the ordination of a ministerial intern for a similar period of time, presumably because he could.

I enjoyed my time as a fledgling pastor. In my initial introduction to the work world after leaving grammar school, I had sat in the Dickensian setting of a stockbroking office behind a desk and being closely directed what to do. Now, I was self-directed. I was in charge of directing the church in my capacity as chair of the church board. I brought all of my education, skills, and innate abilities to bear on my work. I oversaw the various ministry teams of the church comprised of volunteers from the membership. I was responsible for the physical plant and ensuring that the means and the manpower were available to make it function and not fall into disrepair. Working closely with the church treasurer, I monitored the financial health of the church and made sure we operated within budget.

Perhaps my most visible function as a pastor was to preach a sermon every Saturday, which for us was the Sabbath. This was a creative enterprise in the sense that one had to study passages from the Bible, research them thoroughly to establish their context, and extract and then present principles to live by to the congregation in a way that was captivating and did not lull people to sleep. It was a rigorous but rewarding job that bore fruit in member expressions of gratitude for the messages they felt were uplifting and helped them live fulfilled lives. At times, others who were not members committed to the mission of our church by becoming members through baptism by immersion.

I wasn't bound by a nine-to-five routine as I had been in my first jobs. My time was my own to direct and I enjoyed the independence. It actually made me work longer hours than a nine to five would have. I had more of a personal stake in the outcomes I was working to achieve. A growing, thriving church would reflect well on me. I was on call and accessible to members who had issues that needed to be dealt with at all hours of the day and all days of the week—so much so that not long after I started working as a pastor, I began to take Mondays off and devote that day to self-care by going to the gym, pottering around the home or garden, or doing home repairs.

The churches to which I was assigned tended to have mostly Black members and I was embraced and respected by them. I felt a sense of belonging that I hadn't had in other occupations up to that point. However, the longer I worked as a pastor for the Church, the satisfaction I felt working with church members was not a feeling that emerged in my association with the Conference and the way it functioned. Leadership at the conference level appeared to be concerned more with numbers joining the Church through baptism, with offerings and tithe figures collected at the local church, and with the amounts collected for charity projects in a process known as 'ingathering.' Ingathering took place over a period of a few weeks where members were encouraged to go out and knock on doors to solicit donations from households and businesses for disaster relief and community projects in mostly Third World countries.

At the end of each ingathering campaign, champion individual collectors were recognized and lauded. Churches that collected the most were applauded and given kudos for their efforts. The monies collected were undoubtedly for good causes and the public was always told that administrative expenses were low and the rest of the money was not used for the denomination. However, there were rumours about "ingathering reversion funds," a strange, murky practice that appeared to involve money collected above ingathering goals or targets reverting or remaining in the country in which it was collected.

One conference president even called me at home to remonstrate with me about what he perceived as the low amounts my members were collecting for ingathering. I countered, somewhat sharply as I recall, with the fact that my membership numbers were going up as well as the amounts my members were giving in tithe donations. The conversation irritated me immensely, especially since I felt like I was doing a good job with a thriving congregation. At no time prior to that, nor since that time, in my capacity as a church pastor did he ever call to ask how I was doing, encourage me, or offer any other kind of assistance.

Still, my feelings didn't affect my personal faith. I reasoned that the conference president was only human with human foibles and the human penchant for doing whatever he could to advance his own career in the hierarchy of the Church. I maintained my belief in God as the anchor of my life's journey, enabling me to meet the challenges that I faced–a sentiment that remains with me to the present day.

# ELUSIVE SEARCH FOR A HOME

The urge to own my own home was something that, although never overtly expressed, was one I had internalized from watching the drive of my parents to escape what they perceived to be the shackles of the vagaries of landlords and rents. They were hemmed in by the restrictions of not being able to decorate where they lived and put their own stamp on those homes. My parents had to contend with other renters in the same house and the inevitable conflicts that arose, despite their strenuous efforts to avoid confrontation. There weren't many such incidents as I recall, but the irritation of the restrictions and the confrontations were enough to propel my parents into home ownership. Their drive became my own, reinforced by years that followed my return to the UK of moving from one rental property to another.

Another factor in wanting our own home was the birth of our first child, Hermione, in August of 1986. I was overjoyed when, at her birth, I saw her poking out with a full head of curly black hair. Alas, my paltry income as a minister, compounded by Joy not working outside of the home and instead taking care of Hermione in those early years, meant that the banks would not risk advancing us a mortgage to enable us to buy a home. Consequently, Joy and I moved from rental to rental–first from Norbury to Enfield, then to Barnet and Watford.

One major irritant involved having to ask for permission from my employer, the SEC, and specifically the conference treasurer, to rent any particular property. At one point, we found a beautiful place in Bounds Green (an area in which my mother currently resides). The house had been completely renovated by a gentleman who did so for his daughter and her husband to be. Their relationship had sadly ended and the marriage didn't take place. So now, it was available for rent. Everything was new. The fixtures and fittings were immaculate. The walls were tastefully decorated with beautifully designed wallpaper fashionable at the time in the UK. The flooring was new. It was a gorgeous place that Joy and I thought we would find comfortable and met our standards.

We took the description of the place to Conference Treasurer Basil Powell, a Welshman who had spent time as a missionary in Africa before returning to the UK. We required his permission since the conference would be giving us an allowance toward the rental cost. Basil read the description of the property, which was listed as a "luxury" property. Although within the range of what the conference typically approved, he denied us permission to rent it. We were astounded and profoundly disappointed. He argued that the members would be affronted if they knew that their pastors were "living in luxury accommodation." To our minds, the owner, wishing to make his property as marketable as possible, had injected that word in the description of the house and that one word put it out of our reach. It was a bitter decision for us that added to a growing feeling of resentment about the way the Church functioned as an employer.

This decision added to a visit of the conference president and his wife to our home one Saturday, a few months prior to the birth of our first child. We fed Dr. Silburn Reid and Mrs. Leila Reid a sumptuous Sabbath meal. Dr. Reid had preached at my church earlier that day and conventional Adventist hospitality meant we would invite him and his wife home for lunch. We were in a tiny home and we pointed out how small it was and how with a baby on the way, we would like more spacious accommodation. We were sure, perhaps naïvely, that he and his wife would see the logic of our need and that Dr. Reid would put a good word in for us with the Treasurer to approve the accommodation we wanted. We were shocked when they oohed and ahhed about how lovely our home was and saw nothing wrong with it.

## PROMOTION UP THE LADDER

By August of 1986, some major events had happened to project me onto an even higher plane. I say higher plane, but there are some in the Church who would have you believe that working in a local church is the highest calling a minister can have. Yet there is an unspoken, universally acknowledged perception that working in a local conference, or what we call "union" conference, and division or "General Conference" is a promotion up the career ladder.

One major event was my ordination in Coventry at a significant constituency meeting of the Seventh-day Adventist Church. Joy was proudly pregnant with Hermione, who was born just a few months later. Another major event was that so-called higher plane of appointment as the youth director of the SEC. Up to that point, there had always been one youth director for the SEC. Now, I was chosen to be the youth director with a special focus on the London area, where the churches were almost all Black. Another man who was White, Paul Tompkins, was also chosen to be an SEC youth director with a special focus for the provinces, meaning anywhere outside London where the churches were predominantly White. So now, there were two youth directors operating side by side: one for London and one for what was referred to as "the provinces," meaning regions outside of London.

The insidious intrusion of the shadow reached here, too. There were stories that came out in later years of certain White SEC department leaders' and officers' housing being gutted, with dumpsters outside their houses seen receiving the debris to make way for new furniture and fittings. My requests to upgrade the rental property owned by the SEC, where I and my family lived, fell on deaf ears and minor work appeared to be grudgingly approved.

## WORK AS AN EDITOR

In time, I also became communication director for the SEC. One of my talents came to the fore. At Newbold College about seven years earlier, I had been the editor of a paper called *Prism*. In previous years, as its name implies, the paper had been somewhat heady and, in my opinion, pseudo-scholarly. I wanted it to be more down to earth, talking about issues to which students could relate, including life on campus. Barney Allen-Mersh, one of my staff writers, wrote a brilliantly humorous piece in one issue criticizing the endless use of an introit titled "God Be in My Head" that the college choir sang at the beginning of every single Saturday worship service. His acerbic wit was the talk of students and I guess the staff as well, and it probably stung the hapless choir director, Roy Scarr. The following Saturday, the introit was replaced by another one and constantly changed thereafter. Another staff writer, Janice Lowry, wrote equally

brilliant articles. It was a job I loved doing under the guiding spon-
sorship of a staff member named Jonquil Hole. I got a kick out of
seeing students eagerly picking up their copy of *Prism* and devouring
its contents.

Affirmation of the job I was doing at Newbold College came in a letter
to the editor that we published from Stuart R. Ware, who at the time was
the SEC Youth and Family Life Director. He wrote:

> Having just finished reading the article on Race Relations in the Church in
> Prism, I must say that I am greatly encouraged to see it openly discussed in
> such a way ... For the next few years there are bound to be problems in the
> area of race-relations in our church. However if this drive to understand one
> another continues amongst the Newbold Students then I believe we are on
> the way to really seeing our work move forward in Britain.

Evidently, Pastor Ware was expressing his pleasure at seeing a process
at work that had been missing in the Church in those days. My newsletter
contained an open discussion. Back then (and still today), the Seventh-day
Adventist Church avoided open discussions about issues of conflict in
the church in its official communications, preferring to paper over any
perceived cracks. This stems from a belief that the Church has been
especially called by God in what are seen to be "the last days," that it
strives to be pure, and that any negative stories detract from an image
of a Church ready for the Second Coming of Jesus Christ. As a result,
independent journals have emerged, such as *Spectrum* magazine and
*Adventist Today*, that have open discussions about topics to do with
religious and traditional practices within the Church, socio-economics,
and issues of race, gender, and politics as well as theology.

I subsequently became the editor of the Andrews University Theological Seminary newsletter, but it didn't give me the same charge as editing *Prism*. That student group there wasn't as cohesive and close as the Newbold students.

My appointment as SEC communication director in 1986 gave me the opportunity to capitalize on my talent as an editor. The SEC didn't have its own newspaper. It relied on the newspaper of the higher umbrella organization, the British Union Conference's *Messenger*, to get its information out to the membership. This was somewhat unwieldy, with information about SEC events coming out many months after they happened. I decided we needed our own paper that would be nimbler in its dissemination of information about conference activities, keep members in touch with each other, and feature relevant human-interest stories. Especially important to me was the opportunity it would give to the conference, which had a Black president who presided over a predominantly Black membership, to voice its unique opinions, concerns, and flavour. Its official name was the *South England Conference Communicator: Quarterly Newssheet of the South England Conference of the Seventh-day Adventist Church*. We just referred to it as the *Communicator*.

I decided to have a special issue that highlighted the history of the conference. It was an anniversary special highlighting the years 1888 to 1988. I called upon various writers to contribute what they knew about how the Seventh-day Adventist Church started and developed in South England. My home church, the Holloway Church situated in North London opposite the Nags Head pub, featured prominently as one of the first churches established in South England. Pastor Martin Anthony,

Photo of Officers and Directors of the South England Conference of Seventh-day Adventists in the late 1980s, a testament to the successful struggle in the 1970s spearheaded by the London Laymen's Forum for integration of Blacks and Whites in church leadership. Standing from left to right: Marcus Dove, Treasurer; Martin Anthony, Executive Secretary; Cecil Perry, President; Lionel Acton-Hubbard, Health Director; Hymers Wilson (me) Youth & Communication Director. Front row from left to right: David Noel; Roy Chisholm, Publishing. Director; Theodore Sergeant, Personal Ministries Director; Paul Tompkins, Youth Director.

a White Englishman, wrote from his sources and memory of how the "work" started in a piece titled "Celebrating Our History."[13] He and others, such as Dr. Jonathan Gallagher and Pastor W. J. Newman, supplied additional articles along with black-and-white photographs of the White members who pioneered the Seventh-day Adventist Church in England.

---

13. *South England Conference Communicator* 5 (December 1988): 1.

A South Asian minister, Pastor P. G. Mathews, wrote about the history of Asian members in the SEC.

I wrote a piece that I carefully titled "Seventh-day Adventists Lead the Way"[14] so as not to be provocative. I had learned from reading Hemingway as a boy about the power of the written word and here was my opportunity to exercise that power myself. I remembered well how I had been so captivated by Hemingway's written word in his book *The Old Man and the Sea* that I lost all perspective about where I was. Its powerful message of sheer grit had remained with me until the present time and I believed my own words could also have an impact. In my article in the *Communicator*, I recounted the arrival of Black members predominantly from the West Indies in the 1950s among what is commonly known as the Windrush generation. I mentioned the racial conflict in the wider society and racial tensions that began to emerge in the Church. The main point of the piece was to highlight the solution to racial tensions in the Church in which Adventists appeared to be leading the way to reconciliation by forging a system where Black and White leadership could be chosen to work together and where Black ministers could be brought in to fill the gaps that existed.

I was surprised at the severe backlash my piece sparked. My telling of the history of Black Adventists in the South England territory was not welcome by the White church leadership despite the article featuring the boldness of an experiment in shared leadership between Blacks and Whites–something that has not been possible in the Adventist

---

14. Ibid, 6.

Church in many places in the United States to this very day (as an aside, I fully believe that regional Black conferences in the United States worked extremely well for the Black Adventist work there. They may have worked well in the UK if this had been forced on the Black membership).

I never heard specific reasons why the article wasn't welcome, but I speculate that the reaction could have been due to my reference to the initial resistance of Church leadership to the idea of Blacks and Whites sharing leadership roles. I also said the change allowing Blacks to join in leadership that occurred "did not take place without a bitter struggle."[15] Perhaps most galling was my veiled reference to the fact that "human relations among [the Seventh-day Adventist Church] have been far from perfect ... "[16] Understand this against the backdrop of the fact that the Seventh-day Adventist Church has tended, especially in the past, to see itself as a pure group of people who are head and shoulders above others in their standards of morality, healthy lifestyle practices, and under-standing of the Christian scriptures. A dyed-in-the-wool Seventh-day Adventist would say "we have the truth," implying that other faith traditions do not. Even today, reports about errant Church officials or negative events such as the Church being on the losing end of lawsuits can only be found in independent magazines such as *Spectrum* and *Adventist Today* that pride themselves on being free from official church control to publish church issues, warts and all. You would hardly ever read about those things in the *Adventist Review*, the official Seventh-day Adventist paper.

---

15. Ibid.
16. Ibid.

My boss, Pastor Cecil Perry, the then-SEC president, received complaints about my article from Pastor Martin Anthony, Executive Secretary of the British Union Conference of Seventh-day Adventists, and from Ray Dabrowski, Communication Director at the umbrella organization of the Trans European Division of Seventh-day Adventists. Pastor Perry mentioned these complaints to me and decided to mandate that I work with an editorial committee, presumably to ensure I didn't ruffle any more feathers with *Communicator* content. I complied with one meeting of the editorial committee but after realizing how unwieldy and hampering it was, I called no other meetings and produced the next issues without consulting it. I received no questions afterwards about whether or not it was functioning.

Incidentally, the January 1990 *Communicator* issue featured an article by Dr. Andrea Luxton, who had been a fellow student with me at Newbold College and was at the time a senior lecturer at the College. Dr. Luxton was also a member of the SEC Executive Committee. Her article was titled "The Role of Women in SEC Ministry." She wrote about the absence of the input of women in ministry as a "problem" and the fact that " ... this means that the differing insights [women] have are often not heard." Dr. Luxton said she " ... avoided giving her personal conclusions in this paper ... "[17]

Thirty-two years later, with the issue of the ordination of women still unresolved in the Seventh-day Adventist Church, Dr. Luxton, now President of Andrews University in Berrien Springs, Michigan, is a more

---

17. *South England Conference Communicator* 9 (January 1990): 1.

outspoken advocate of women's ordination. I mention this as an inci-
dental story, but it really isn't. The shadow of male headship, an integral
part of secular and religious American society that has contributed to
the fuelling of racism, has also negatively impacted Black and White
women (with Black women bearing the brunt, it must be said).

The reaction to my article illustrates an endemic problem in the
Seventh-day Adventist Church. I would like to experience a church and
society free from sexism and racism, where the contributions of all races
and genders are equally respected and rewarded. Who wouldn't? Former
Canadian Prime Minister Pierre Trudeau once famously said, "The
government has no business in the bedrooms of the nation." Likewise,
I believe the Church has no business in the bedrooms of its members. I
believe the Church exists to care in tangible ways for people of all
persuasions, regardless of their sexual orientation. The problem is the
Church does not appear to have the stomach for an open discussion
about issues that threaten to expose it as less than pure and perfect. It is
an endemic blight that perpetuates a slavish hold on the status quo and
a hankering by some in high positions in the church to go back to the
way things functioned in the late nineteenth century. It is a blight experienced in the wider so-called First World society where, in some
quarters, the excesses of past colonialism and their enduring effects on
the colonized and the benefits that continue to accrue for former colonial
powers are suppressed and waved away as matters that threaten a seemingly peaceful status quo.

So rather than embrace my article stating how the Church in South
England, through a struggle, paved the way to Blacks and Whites sharing

leadership at the highest level in the conference, there was backlash and recrimination. But the 'damage' was already done: the article was out there. It was being read and doing its thing of stirring minds and challenging the status quo.

# A NEW HOME COUNTRY
## A RAY OF SUNSHINE

A year and eight months after the issue surrounding the article I published in the *Communicator*, I, my wife Joy, and my two daughters Hermione and Hannah, who was born in 1988, were on a plane heading to Canada. We were leaving the UK for good and beginning a new life with hopefully better economic prospects. I was frankly somewhat tired of church work so, after establishing residence in Canada, Joy's home country, we were heading to Kettering Medical Center (KMC) near Dayton, Ohio, where I was going to do a one-year clinical pastoral education program, training to become a hospital chaplain, beginning in August 1991.

My brother-in-law George and my wife's sister Wilma (Dale) drove me and my family to Kettering, Ohio, in their Mazda van. Through UPS, we had sent ahead seven suitcases with our personal belongings. We arrived in Kettering, got the keys to the house we would be renting for the year, and got settled in.

A couple of days later, I went to report to where I was going to receive my training. I had no vehicle, but KMC was close to where we were living so it was going to take me about half an hour to walk there.

On the way, a White man driving by saw me and offered me a ride. We struck up a conversation. He was curious about what brought me to those parts. It turned out he was working at KMC as a doctor. I told him I had come from Canada, I was in Kettering with my wife and family, and I had literally just arrived. I told him I had come to KMC to train as a chaplain.

What happened next has stayed with me for the rest of my life. It happened on a Friday. That man told me he was going for a short weekend trip with his wife and kids out of town and wouldn't be needing his car. He told me I could use it and return it on Sunday evening.

I have often asked myself since then, "Who does that?" The man gave me a ride to his house, gave me the keys to his car, and allowed me, a complete stranger, to use it for that whole weekend. With that car, I was able to get the rest of the way to my orientation at KMC. I was able to buy enough groceries for my family to last until I could purchase a car of my own. I was also able to take the family to our first church service there. I was so grateful for the loan of that vehicle. It helped us to get on our feet in Kettering. It turned what could have been a difficult and stressful first few days into a smoother transition into life there.

When it was time to return the car, I had a problem. I couldn't remember the name of the man who had lent me his car. I couldn't even clearly remember where he lived. For a while there, I was in panic mode because I wasn't sure how I would get the car back to the owner. Fortunately, I eventually remembered where the house was and returned both the car and the keys. I still don't remember the man's name and I've often thought I would love to thank him again, in person, for his kindness.

I have had situations like these that have brought a measure of balance into my worldview. There are kind people in every group. Most White people have been socialized with expectations of being on its top rungs over any other people of colour and with a sense of entitlement to achieve whatever society offers without fear or favour. Consequently, the actions of White people in many cases are shaped by their socialization. There are many who have slighted me with their actions, unaware of our shared history with its painful past mired in ideas of Manifest Destiny, slavery, and their ripple effects felt to this very day. But I have also met many very kind and thoughtful White people who, in spite of their upbringing, have taken the time to listen and be informed about the realities of racism. They have engaged me with mutual respect and empathy.

## TRAINING TO BE A CHAPLAIN

As I settled into my training at the Clinical Pastoral Education (CPE) program, I realized what an eye-opener it would be. The training was nothing like what I had encountered at the Andrews Theological Seminary. I was challenged to look within the deepest, darkest places of my psyche and verbally express my feelings. I had been brought up in England and, unlike Americans, we were not accustomed to blurting out what was going on inside our heads. I used to marvel at Americans on television telling anybody who wanted to hear about how great they were at this or that, and how they were the best and most suited to whatever demands were at hand. I was used to being self-deprecating. I downplayed my achievements and frankly, I wasn't even aware of my gifts. As the training continued, that changed and I began to be more aware of my gifts and capabilities. CPE helped me to begin to express and air my thoughts about myself. I became more aware of and able to define my feelings. I was more easily touched by human tragedy, and I found tears welled more easily in my eyes as tragic situations presented themselves to me.

My training involved didactics (Americans love grand-sounding names for stuff), which was group instruction and times for sharing our experiences that included our thoughts and feelings about our encounters with patients on the hospital units. There were six of us trainee chaplains in the program: me, Trish, Fred, Raul, Warren, and one other man, a part-time Baptist minister whose name I can't recall. Our chaplain supervisor was Rev. Henry Uy, a Filipino American who I played ping pong with after work hours but was never able to beat. The harder I played and the more energetic my shots, the greater the ease with which he would match them. I would finish the games all hot and flustered while he didn't break a sweat. He was like a Zen master. He told me he was just absorbing my energy.

In the afternoons, we trainee chaplains received a census list containing the names and locations of patients on the units. We would then go talk to them and comfort them. We were trained to meet the spiritual needs of anyone, regardless of their faith tradition. We were even sensitive to the needs of those with no faith tradition, who were not religious at all. I even ministered to a woman who said she was a Wiccan!

I had heard about people from the Appalachians. They had a reputation for being rugged, not very educated, and dyed-in-the-wool rednecks. My experiences meeting the family members of their deceased loved ones were positive. As a chaplain, I would be the first to call them into the hospital. We would never say over the telephone what the issue was; all we would say is that it was urgent. When they arrived, I would greet them and let them know their family member had passed away. Their reactions were varied, but most were appreciative of my words of comfort and prayers. Many just hugged me and received the comfort of the embrace that we shared.

## REALITY CHECK

The time came when my thoughts turned to going beyond just taking the training and now pursuing a career in chaplaincy. I loved the work. I wanted to continue as a chaplain. A job posting came up for a chaplain position at the KMC. I applied. I felt comfortable at the interview. My ten years of experience as an ordained minister, five years in local churches in London and five years working in the SEC as a youth director as well as communications and Sabbath School (similar to Sunday School) director, I felt were impressive. But then came the question from Ron Gordon, the Director of Chaplaincy and a White man: "Many of our patients are Appalachians. Do you feel comfortable working with them?"

I was taken aback by the question. We both knew, and the other members of the interview panel knew, what he meant. I was Black. The Appalachians were White and supposedly rednecks. How would I manage relating to them? I calmly told him and the other interviewers that I had encountered no negative issues working with Appalachian patients or family members. I found them to be friendly and accommodating. I didn't mention that I had attended grammar school in the UK where I was one of three Black boys in my cohort year in a school that had an enrollment of 600. I had grown up as a minority among White people from elementary school until I attended South Bank Polytechnic in my early 20s. Maybe I should have told them.

The job went to my friend Raul Concha, whose father-in-law was a physician currently working at KMC. Raul wasn't yet ordained and he had only a few short years working as a church pastor in Nevada. He also didn't have the experience of working as a conference departmental head as I had. When I asked Ron Gordon why I hadn't gotten the job, he said, "You didn't look hungry enough for the job." I wonder whether it would have made any difference if I had been more demonstrative about my passion to be a chaplain. But I do recall that the interview was overshadowed by Gordon's question of whether, as a Black man, I'd be able to minister to Appalachians. I am convinced that this and nepotism, not my apparent lack of desire, were the real reasons why I didn't get the job.

I gave up on the idea of staying and working in the United States. A friend who had entered illegally tried to tell me how easy it would be to remain in the States, operating under the radar and eventually transitioning to legitimate residency. I decided that to do so with my wife and three children was too risky. Our third child, Hymers III, had been born during my time training as a chaplain at KMC in April 1992, and the presence of our precious newborn made it imperative for both Joy and me that we made the right moves. The prospect of jumping nervously at every knock on our door as an illegal immigrant did not fill me with any enthusiasm. I had no stomach for that kind of existence, so we headed back to Canada where I had every right to be, armed with my residence permit.

In any case I had come from the United Kingdom a year earlier and that in itself was quite an achievement. I had left a full-time job as a minister. My job was a conference job, recognized as a promotion in Adventist circles. I had left a house that Joy, I, and the bank owned. But I had left it all looking for greener pastures overseas, and Canada was going to be that place where we would make a better life for us and our children. Still, there was no job waiting for either me or Joy in Canada. We had gone to Ohio with eight suitcases, and we were re-entering Canada with a small rental truck full of new possessions.

## PUTTING DOWN CANADIAN ROOTS: OTTAWA

Our first place was Joy's mother's home on 201 Hinton Avenue in Ottawa. Our entire family–our two daughters Hermione and Hannah, and our four-month-old son Hymers III–slept in my mother-in-law's attic. Gran Gran, as we called her, allowed us use of the kitchen and living room.

I had to look for work. The responsibility of providing for my family weighed heavily on me, but I don't remember feeling at all worried about it. I found an employment agency and got my very first job, which involved a one-night gig as a waiter at a fundraiser for Bosnian Relief on Parliament Hill. The year was 1992 and it was an adventure. I remember enjoying the fun of waiting tables, seeing people dressed to the hilt and meeting a tall, well-built Canadian girl who waited tables with me and with whom I developed a nice camaraderie. I never saw her again, but she was a refreshing example of young people who grab the meagre opportunities that exist to pay their bills and put food on the table. I say 'refreshing' because I had been a high-flying church man, a pastor, and department director delivering sermons, running workshops and retreats, and editing a newsletter read by thousands of church members in southern England. I had mixed almost exclusively with church people and had recognition. Now, here I was in relative obscurity waiting tables with down-to-earth Canadians, trying to eke out an existence in what we now call the gig economy.

My second job lasted two months and saw me working for the federal government at Consulting and Audit Canada. This office monitored and approved government employee per diem and travel expenses. There were consultants in that office who drafted numerous papers on all kinds of subjects, many of which, I fancy, collected dust in various government offices. I could only get contract positions with the Feds because I was only a permanent resident, otherwise known as a landed immigrant. I can't even remember what my task was there. I certainly wasn't at a level to approve expenses. Nor was I a consultant, although I observed with interest and envy the excitement of the bright, mainly young, consultants seeing the boxes of manuscripts they had written and leafing through the pages that had caused so many sleepless nights and nervous energy as they sweated and struggled to meet production deadlines. Permanent jobs were reserved for Canadian citizens.

I remember Hallowe'en at Consulting and Audit Canada. It was my first time seeing how Canadians celebrate that event. Actually, people in the UK didn't celebrate it at all as far as I knew. In any case, I wouldn't really know, having worked in a church environment that would have regarded Hallowe'en as Satanic at worst and as a Catholic tradition to be shunned at best. People came to work that day dressed in various outfits–some as witches, others in other creative and amusing outfits. One young woman even came as Catwoman complete with a tail!

All too soon, my time at Consulting and Audit Canada came to an end. My employment agency sent me to work at Transport Canada. My boss was Stan Linnen, a dour man with an accent that I was informed was uniquely Ottawa Valley. We sat in rows in a somewhat Dickensian setting, with Stan at the head of the room facing us, his minions, all seated facing him. My job was to find missing files. When I was first given the task, there were several pages of missing files. I worked steadily at finding them in various parts of the building on Slater Street and even in places off-site, such as storage areas in Tunney's Pasture. I was proud that when I left the job, I had reduced the list of missing files to half a page. Along with my cleanup of a stationery cupboard, this achievement didn't go unnoticed. There was a discussion among the supervisors about keeping me on, but I had been offered a position by the Ontario Conference of Seventh-day Adventists to be the principal and a teacher at a small Seventh-day Adventist Church school. I jumped at it because it gave Joy and I the opportunity, with its salary, to afford to rent a townhouse in Kanata and leave Gran Gran's attic so generously given to us to live when we arrived in Canada from Ohio.

Alas, this improvement in our financial fortunes would come at a high price. 1993 to 1994 would turn out to be the worst year of my life up to that point, with the shadow again rearing its ugly head–this time at this tiny Seventh-day Adventist school.

There were approximately thirty-four children at the school, from first to eighth grades. Of these 34, only about 8 were White. There were three teachers: Joy Brown, Reema Sukumaran (nee Dixit) and me. I was the principal, but also taught five grades, from grade four to eight. I taught all subjects, English, math, and so on. in one room. I was new to this world although I had taught Religious Knowledge to single grades previously at John Loughborough School in North London. I had some preparation given to me by having travel, tuition and board paid to attend Canadian Union College (now called Berman University) in Alberta, doing courses designed to begin to prepare me to be a teacher. Even so, I found myself preparing classes day by day for the next day's classes, working late into each night to get them done. Our family time suffered. I had no life that school year.

There's a lot I could say about that experience, but I'm sticking to what overshadowed everything else. In addition to us three teachers, there was a woman who was Jewish who came in on a part-time basis to teach French. One day, she came to me, as principal, and suggested I organize a Black History Month focus for the school in February 1994 that would recognize the achievements of Black luminaries such as Dr. Martin Luther King, Jr., Frederick Douglass, Elijah McCoy, Mary Seacole, and Rosa Parks, to name a few. It was a suggestion that made consummate sense to me, given the makeup of the student population.

We put pictures of the Black luminaries up on the school hallway walls with brief descriptions of their achievements. Our goal was to visually educate all our pupils, Black and White, and to also instill a sense of pride in our Black pupils–one that has generally been missing in the Black community.

Before the month was up, someone (we think one of the church members) had ripped down the pictures off the walls. In addition, parents began withdrawing their White children from the school until none were left. No reasons for the withdrawals were given by the parents. There was nothing verbally or in writing. In the first semester, some-where around November 1993, I had a glowing performance review by Assistant Education Superintendent of the Ontario Conference of Seventh-day Adventists Dave Higgins. By March 1994, Higgins did a follow-up performance review that completely reversed the findings of his first one. In the first review, I was delivering classroom instruction effectively, classroom management was good, and students were learning. Now he had nothing good to say about instruction, management, or the way the children were learning. I marvelled at how this could have happened and concluded it had nothing to do with my efforts in the classroom, but everything to do with the decline in enrollment because of Black History Month.

I remember the blow to my ego in this situation. I had previously thought I could do anything with hard work and dedication. I could do anything, learn anything, tackle any job; just give me time and the opportunity. I had observed my parents and their determination to make ends meet and provide for me and my sisters. Hard work and a sense of duty compelled them. My father told me that if you do a job, do it well. I adopted these values. They worked for my parents and they would work for me. Up to that point, in fact, they *had* worked for me. I had been a successful church pastor. I had earned my stripes by transitioning smoothly from being a licensed minister to being ordained and I had been promoted to the level of a conference director.

But this job proved to undo my self-confidence. My contract was terminated. I left with my sense of self in tatters. I had failed. For the first time in my working life, I had been fired. I was devastated. When I would tell my side of the story to the few people in whom I confided, tears flowed easily—far too easily I thought. I was extremely fragile at that time. I had been shaken to the core.

I also remember performing a somewhat symbolic act of shaving my hair down to nearly bald almost as a way of divesting myself of the horrible past year and the beginnings of a process of reinventing myself. Yet re-finding my strength and resilience didn't come as quickly as that act. Moments like this in life have tested me to my limit. I can't say my mental fortitude was always as strong as it should be. The tears that came all too easily were evidence of that, but it did help me immensely to know I wasn't alone in my struggle. My wife Joy was uncompromisingly supportive as she always was, and it kept me going knowing she had my back. I prayed a lot at that time too. Turning to a Higher Power for a way through what I was experiencing was in my DNA. I had been brought up to rely on supernatural aid when faced with circumstances beyond my control. It was the go-to solution for my parents before me. It had worked for them. From all accounts, our forebears before them had endured the inexplicably horrendous dark night of slavery and emerged as a people, as survivors. I prayed for God to just help me get through the darkness of that moment and give me the mental muscle to carry the psychological burden of what I was going through. Nevertheless, it would take a while before I could dig deep myself out of the mental abyss in which I now found myself.

## MOVING TO MOOSE FACTORY

The termination of my employment at the school was a curious affair. The school board, made up of members of the Ottawa Seventh-day Adventist Church and surrounding Adventist churches, said the Ontario Conference of Seventh-day Adventists was recommending my termination. However, the Ontario Conference Education department said it was the school board that was recommending my termination. I found it interesting that neither entity wanted to take responsibility for getting rid of me.

At any rate, it was time to move on. But the termination was recommended in March or April 1994 to take effect at the end of the school year, in June 1994, so I still had a few months left to work. Looking back, I often think I should have dropped everything there and then and just walked out, leaving the kids, parents, and church to figure out how to finish out the school year. Somehow, through the prayers and Joy's support, I found a way to carry on even though I felt like a reject and was a shadow of my formerly confident self. The sense of duty instilled in me by my parents and my English grammar school education compelled me to stay on–and yes, I still had rent to pay. So, maybe that decision wasn't all about duty to the children. But a big part of it must have been duty to my family to keep my pay coming in to cover our bills.

It did all have to end eventually anyway and as fortune would have it, Joy got a job in Moose Factory with the Mushkegowuk Council that paid significantly more money than I had been earning. The Mushkegowuk Council is a non-political Chiefs Council that provides support services to eight First Nations communities. She left in May 1994 for her position as a diabetes coordinator up at the southern tip of James Bay. She would provide diabetes education promoting better health outcomes for the Indigenous people. I finished out my contract toward the end of June 1994, working at the school for what seemed like an eternity while parenting our children on my own. Then, the kids and I rejoined Joy in Moose Factory right after I completed my time at the school.

We then spent just over nine months in Moose Factory, where I became a house husband. I had worked any chance I got since I was in my teens, but now the words "knowledge of Cree is essential" on job listings I saw while in that Indigenous community blocked any thoughts I may have had of getting a job of my own there. Not that it was all bad. The time off from working gave me opportunities for emotional healing from what I had experienced at the Ottawa Adventist school. I was able to be involved in looking after my children in a way that probably wouldn't have otherwise been available to me. I potty-trained my son and saw my children off to the local Ministik public school each morning. I would pull my son on a little sled around on the snow until one day a pack of dogs became interested in the little human, and one dog got close enough to tug on his parka with its teeth presumably with plans of a tasty meal. That was it for me. I got him off the sled and we never did that again. To break up these packs, there would be periodic culls of the stray dogs where dog owners were warned ahead of time to secure their animals and keep them inside while the cull was going on.

Then one day, I was walking along the banks of the Muskoka River on my own. It must have been before the snows came, perhaps around late summer or early fall of 1994. It was just me and the sounds of the water lapping the river's edge. I had no job. I couldn't get a job because I didn't speak Cree. Work had defined me up to that point. I was an ordained minister in my previous life. I received recognition and kudos from church members who listened when I spoke in my sermons and at church board and general membership meetings. I had been a conference director travelling all over South England. Members in a multitude of Seventh-day Adventist churches took note of messages I brought them as a preacher and as a representative of the umbrella organization. More recently, I had been an aspiring teacher and a school principal. Now, I was forced to confront who I really was without a job title. I felt like I was nothing. It was a thought I had to deal with later as I redefined myself. But for now, I looked out onto that river and had an overwhelming sense that I had reached rock bottom. I was nobody.

But then amazingly, curiously (and I'm not even sure how to describe it), a transformational and redeeming thought pushed itself onto my consciousness as I meandered along the Muskoka riverbank. I was at rock bottom, yes, but everything from here would, by definition, be up! I had a strong sense that things couldn't get worse. Looking back, I'd have to say that this was the initiation of a transformation for me. Although fuzzy and indistinct, it was there nonetheless, and I began to see myself in different terms: I was a father, a husband, a person who was loved and appreciated by my family. I was a person of value who was currently in a valley, but heading in a direction that was moving upwards. I didn't know where or how, but I knew the trajectory could in no way be heading down. So, no, my Moose Factory experience was by no means all bad.

Living on the island of Moose Factory among the Indigenous people was an education. It was different to anything I had experienced before. One evening, I was looking out of my front window and saw a huge dog jump into a pickup parked outside and jump back out dragging the carcass of some animal, probably a deer, held firmly in its jaws. I marvelled at the powerful strength of that dog. Another thing new to me was that on New Year's Eve, the assistant chief, who lived next door to us, would go out onto his porch with his family and friends and shoot rounds from a rifle into the air, heralding the New Year. I had never seen these kinds of things in Highbury, North London, where I grew up.

Our family developed our own traditions in this new place. On Saturday afternoons, we would go for walks on the snow-covered dirt roads that were ploughed and packed down after each snowfall. Although it was cold, our parkas, Sorel boots, and heavy-duty mittens defied the elements, and we enjoyed the feel of the crisp, untainted air and the satisfying crunch of the snow underfoot.

We only knew one other person in Moose Factory, Joseph Roberts, who came from South London, and who was the husband of the woman who had recruited Joy for the job of Diabetes Coordinator in her place while she took time off from the community. I knew him through his sister, who I had met years before in North London when she was training to be a nurse. Other than our association with Joseph, we weren't close to the Indigenous people who lived on the island. We met some of them through Joseph and Joy knew others through working for the Mushke-gowuk Council, but we felt like outsiders there. Spending some of our free time with Joseph, a fellow Londoner who we easily related to, helped us get through our time in the community.

Family friends with whom we have remained connected since the 1980s. Pictured: Parents Halsey (left) and Marisol Peat (right) with their children Dina (left) and An-nia (right). Halsey sent cassette tapes and letters to us while we were living in Moose Factory at the southern tip of James Bay in northern Ontario in 1993/4.

In a time before e-mail was as widely a thing as it is now, we were also buttressed by the cassette tapes of messages our family received from Halsey Peat back in England, who recorded children's stories based on his own childhood for our three kids. Halsey and I exchanged newsletters via what we now call snail mail, humorously documenting, in tabloid fashion, what was happening in our respective locations.

At Christmas in 1994, our isolation was also broken by a visit from Joy's mother, Aldith, who flew into Moosonee Airport. I picked her up from the airport and together we travelled across the frozen Muskoka River to Moose Factory with a local man known as Blue Boy, who pulled a coffin-like structure in which Aldith and I sat, hitched to his snowmobile. On her way back out of the community weeks later, we made the return journey with the ice melting and squishy. Every now and then on the trip across, Blue Boy would stand up on his snowmobile to survey the river ahead of him to make sure we didn't get on to thinner ice than his machine would safely navigate before motoring on a few more feet until we reached the shore on the other side. We reasoned with a sense of sombre comedy that if we did go down, we'd already have a coffin prepared for us.

We may not have been close with any of the Indigenous people on the island but living there was an important education into the dynamics of First Nation life. It wasn't just the way everything on the island seemed to shut down during designated hunting season, where whole families would take off into the bush to hunt caribou, moose, and other animals. The meat gathered in this way was stored in freezers and supplied food for the coming winter. Nor was it merely the bannock, a traditional no-yeast frybread that reminded us of bakes made in

Grenada, where Joy was born, or Johnny cakes made in Jamaica where I was born.

It was more about the way the island had been carved up with one part under the jurisdiction of the Province of Ontario and the other part, a reserve, under the jurisdiction of the Federal Government of Canada. I had come from England and had no idea about the Indigenous people I was encountering in a limited way, so I borrowed a book about their history. I had read extensively about the slavery of Africans, so I was somewhat accustomed to horrific stories of oppression. Now I was exposed to the colonization of the Indigenous people and I wasn't prepared for those horrors. I have to confess that I got about a quarter of my way through the book and had to abandon it. It was too much for me. The sadness of the experience of First Nations and the subjugation of their people by colonial powers was traumatizing for me and added to the already oppressive weight of my own history.

## THE MUSKOKA YEARS

In March 1995, it was time to leave. Joy's contract with the Mushkeg-owuk Council came to an end and although we had planned to leave later, the spring weather had brought on an early thawing of the Moose River. We hastily packed in our car whatever belongings we had not already shipped ahead and drove across the river from Moose Factory to Moosonee, where we were going to catch the Polar Bear Express train to Cochrane. From Cochrane, we would pick up our car from the train transport and drive to Ottawa. We would be able to once again take refuge there at Joy's mother's place on Hinton Avenue while we planned the next steps in our precarious future.

We were eager to get out of Moose Factory. There was no way we could stay there with neither me nor Joy having jobs. We didn't want to be stuck any longer than was absolutely necessary. To delay might mean we would have to wait until the river thawed completely, which could have taken at least until April 1995, then have our car shipped across the river. Taking the risk of driving across a melting river saved us money and time to figure out our next moves on the other side.

Joy had been waiting for a response to a job interview she'd taken at Huntsville Hospital to be Food Service Manager. In the meantime, she had a job offer to be a dietitian from an Indigenous group in Commanda, Ontario. She accepted the offer. We decided we would need to find a place to live in nearby Sturgeon Falls. We called ahead to a property manager there. He was effusive in his report of plenty of prop-erties for rent. Imagine our bewilderment when we arrived, and he saw us and greeted us with the sad news that actually there was just one place he had available. When we saw the house, we realized it was a dump and we left, deflated and bemused about the contrast between the prop-erty manager's earlier report and the grim reality, or so it appeared, that actually there was nothing available for us to live in.

It was another example of the shadowy enemy. Our experience in Sturgeon Falls spoke volumes about the unsuitability of that town for our family as a place to live. The vibe we got was that we were not wanted and we didn't deserve a decent place. The change from the friendliness of that property manager and the promise of properties galore over the telephone to stammering apologies in his presence about the sudden dearth of accommodations could only mean one thing in our minds when we reflected on it later.

As it happens, Joy took the initiative to call Gail Sargeant, who had interviewed her at Huntsville Hospital. We had inexplicably heard nothing about whether Joy had been successful in the interview in the weeks that followed. In our experience, that was never a sign of a positive outcome. Now that the possibility of taking the job in Commanda was evaporating, there was a new do-or-die urgency to find out whether she had the job or it had gone to someone else. Joy got through to Gail and asked her if she had been selected for the food service manager job. Gail paused and we heard later that she went to shut her office door. She came back to the telephone and told Joy that she had indeed interviewed successfully, and the job was hers. Gail explained that she had wanted someone for the position who could take charge and the interview revealed Joy had that capability. We were ecstatic. Joy told the people at Commanda that she had changed her mind. She was no longer going to work there. We never did find out why it took Gail so long to get back to Joy with the results of her interview.

Driving to Huntsville, Ontario, months earlier to attend the interview had been a treat. The landscape was breathtaking. The lush green leafy trees were a contrast to the trees we had seen up in Moose Factory, which were stunted by being rooted in permafrost. Accustomed to receiving tourists to cottage country every summer when the population would triple, the locals in Huntsville were affable and easy-going, at least on the surface, even if it was challenging to be accepted into their inner circles.

By April 1995, just before Joy's birthday and after a hair-raising drive in a car with bald tires in a snowstorm from Ottawa across Algonquin Park on Highway 60, we were back in Huntsville. As we settled in, people in that small town of 14,000 would see us, say "hi," and know immediately that we were the family who had moved into 18 Johanna Street.

It was a great place to bring up our children. We did make a few friends there who we continue to keep in touch. Some of them were work colleagues and others we met at the Seventh-day Adventist Church we attended every Saturday in Bracebridge, just over thirty kilometres from where we lived. We were close to lakes and we could take our kids to play at their beaches. For the first of our summers in Huntsville, it seemed like the sun shone every day and the temperatures soared consistently into the upper 20s Celsius. After work, Joy and I would take the children on a short ride to Kinsmen Beach and we would hang out there, eating pizza we bought from the local Pizza Hut. We did that about twice a week that summer. It was great.

Summers in Muskoka, the region a couple of hours north of Toronto comprised of its three major towns of Gravenhurst, Bracebridge and Huntsville, seemed like the Caribbean–that is, until the experience of following summers made it clear that the typical summer was not as consistently warm. We also enjoyed hiking with the children on trails carved out in the wilds of Algonquin Provincial Park.

Photo of my family: From left to right Hannah, Hermione, Hymers Jr. (me) Joy with Hymers III on her lap.

Coaching son Hymers III's soccer team in Huntsville, Ontario in the late 1990s

In the winters, the children and I learned how to skate at the Centennial Centre's ice rink and downhill ski at the Hidden Valley ski hill. I took up cross-country skiing at Arrowhead Provincial Park. We were closer to nature than I had experienced in my early years growing up in the concrete jungle of Highbury in North London. There was also what I would call the 'ugly' time between the end of the snow in late February and the time the leaves would show on the trees in late May or early June of each year. During that intermediate time, the trees were bare and the landscape dull and grey.

I began to think about what I could do for work in Muskoka. With only my Master of Divinity degree, I believed I would need to go back to school for qualifications that were more marketable. I decided on a strategy of building on what I already had in the way of qualifications. I was already in the helping professions as a minister of religion, so I chose to apply to do a Master of Social Work degree at several Canadian universities and a Master of Counselling Psychology at Wayne State University in Detroit. I was accepted at the University of Toronto (U of T), but they didn't consider my Master of Divinity degree an academic degree and so wanted me to do a four-year Bachelor of Social Work degree followed by a one-year Master of Social Work degree. On the other hand, Wilfrid Laurier University (WLU) in Waterloo, Ontario, was willing to accept my Divinity qualifications and allow me into their two-year Master of Social Work program. I was elated. I would happily do the two-year program to achieve my goal rather than the five years it would have taken me to get there at U of T.

Studying at Wilfrid Laurier University was a major part of my recovery from the trauma of losing my employment with the Ontario Conference as principal and teacher at the Ottawa Seventh-day Adventist Church school. My time in Moose Factory had given me opportunities to reflect on who I was as a person. I would never be the same. Now, I was a student participating in discussions about how people functioned in society and social work traditions of helping those experiencing difficulties of all kinds. I worked on producing term papers in which I explored existing scholarship on social issues and added my own thoughts and conclusions to those issues. I recovered my self-esteem as I began to realize that not only did I have something to say from my vantage point as a mature student, but I was good at it. Thankfully, we didn't have the examinations that had tended to be the bane of my existence in the past. Instead, we produced major term papers for each class

on which we were graded. I received an A for all of them and consequently, the classes that required them. I was ecstatically happy to receive
the hugely affirming "with distinction" on my MSW diploma.

I was no longer the failed teacher or unsuccessful principal. I could
look past the failure and see myself once again as a person of worth. I
had found the resilience deep down that I needed to make a fresh start,
to apply to university, and to find my voice and strengths again. The
epiphany I experienced on the shores of the Muskoka River, informing
me that my life would take an upward trajectory from that point on, had
become a welcome reality.

I was fortunate to do a placement in Muskoka at the Muskoka Parry
Sound Community Mental Health Service (MPSCMHS) in my second
semester at WLU. Charlane Cluett, one of the MPSCMHS managers,
came to Waterloo to interview me for a placement position at a local
pub there. She felt I would be a good fit with my experience as a pastor
already under my belt.

I enjoyed learning the craft of counselling there and for the first
time in my life, I had the sense of doing work I felt uniquely suited
to. I am by nature a people person. I get a charge out of connecting
with those I meet. I like talking to people and hearing their unique
stories and here I was talking to people, listening to and learning about
their situations. Frankly, I was learning about how Canadians think
and conduct themselves in the heartland. It didn't feel like a job. It
didn't involve the kind of multi-tasking of being a pastor, which meant
looking after the physical plant, chairing church boards, visiting

members in their homes to provide spiritual nurture and in hospitals when they got sick, teaching the Bible, baptizing new converts, leading worship services, dedicating babies, officiating at weddings, conducting funerals, and preaching weekly sermons. Being a pastor was more like being the executive director of an agency with additional spiritual care responsibilities thrown in.

In comparison, counselling was less multifaceted. I helped people one-on-one, mostly those with serious mental illnesses such as mood disorders, psychoses, trauma, and relationship issues, to express their challenges. I would assist them in discovering their inner strengths and the resources, both external and internal, to navigate their difficulties. Although I was trained in my Master of Social Work program at university to be judicious in my therapeutic use of self, meaning I had to be cautious about using my own life experiences to help my clients in counselling, I was able to carefully integrate the ideas of strength, resilience, and identity I had learned from my personal journey. I am eternally indebted to Charlane for giving me this opportunity that opened up so much for me in my life from that point on.

I did my second placement at the Muskoka Children's Aid Society. I didn't enjoy it as much and after about half of the time there doing child protection work, I transitioned to adoption disclosure work, matching children who were seeking out their birth parents or the other way around. In some cases, this would lead to bringing the parties together–a job above my pay grade but it was somewhat satisfying to know that this was happening, even though it was a process that took months and even years to finally come to fruition.

Eventually, I was offered part time positions at MPSCMHS, where I had done my first placement, and I settled into being an Adult Protective Service worker, assisting people with developmental disabilities to access generic services. I also worked as a counsellor there. After six years of working, I had done almost all the jobs at the agency–from Adult Protective Service work, counselling, crisis support, and mental health work on an Assertive Community Treatment team to the positions of assistant team leader and an area manager supervising counsellors and crisis support workers. During this time, I also became a Canadian citizen, joining my

Mom and dad Dahlia and Hymers Sr. came to visit us for a year in 1995/6 to help with child care while Joy and I were working.

children who had gotten their citizenships when they were babies through Joy, a citizen since her late teens after arriving from the Caribbean.

I had transitioned away from being a pastor, but I still attended the nearest Seventh-day Adventist Church in Bracebridge. I was happy for the relative anonymity there. Back in the United Kingdom, I was well-known in church circles. Wherever I went, I was addressed as "Pastor." There were expectations of me. In social gatherings, I was always called upon to say grace, a brief prayer to bless the food. Now in the church in Bracebridge, I enjoyed being just another member. I was Hymers again, not a title. That is, until Joy disclosed that I was a pastor after we had been attending for a year. This new information made them push for me to be an elder of the church, a volunteer position that supports the paid minister. I was a little annoyed that my cover, so to speak, was blown, but I soon settled into the role supporting Fred Irish, who was the pastor of that congregation and facilitating a weekly Bible study.

I spent a happy ten years in Huntsville and learned my craft as a counsellor. In my early years after graduating with my MSW, I also had a private practice doing Employee Assistance Program counselling for a company. I was a partner of Nell Thomas in MPS Rehab, which had a contract providing social work, speech and language and, for a brief period, nutrition services for the local Community Care Access Centre, formerly known as Home Care. I had to give up much of my private practice work once I took on more responsibilities at MPSCMHS.

As a counsellor, I did talk therapy with people from all walks of life, including police officers, prison guards, lawyers, retirees, students, corporate business people, and business owners. I also dealt with people who had mood and psychotic issues that exacerbated their abilities to function well in relationships, work, and study.

I learned a lot about the Canadian way of life in cottage country. I learned how to chop logs with a maul for firewood along with the importance of storing them and letting them dry for a whole summer before using them. I learned how to start a fire with birch bark. I learned how to paddle and steer a canoe, including how to use the J stroke. Male prison guards and police officers who I counselled had a tendency to be as controlling of their female partners in their home life as they needed to be on the job, with destructive consequences for their domestic situations. I learned about lawyers and business executives who had issues with procrastination and an inability to shut off work even when on vacation, like anyone else in the other places I had worked. I learned from other residents, who I met at my kids' soccer practices, that the easy-going, friendly nature of cottage country dwellers belied an underlying hesitancy to let strangers into their inner circles even after ten years living in Muskoka. In my case, our church affiliation cushioned our family from that hesitation because we benefited from the acceptance of members who had religious beliefs in common.

By 2004, I was an area manager at Muskoka-Parry Sound Community Mental Health Service. I was supervising eleven employees. Those employees were a mixture of crisis support workers and counsellors. It was an especially busy period at the agency. I was already Area Manager in the Muskoka area, supervising counsellors and crisis support workers

First home Joy and I owned in Canada in Huntsville, Ontario purchased in November 1996

in Gravenhurst, Bracebridge, and Huntsville. The area manager in the Sundridge office went on maternity leave, and I was invited to be the area manager there in her absence. This meant more employees to supervise. On top of the added burden of supervision, there was additional travel. The Bracebridge office where I had Muskoka counsellors and crisis support workers was about 30 kilometres south of my home in Huntsville, and the Sundridge office where I had East Parry Sound employees was about 30 kilometres north of where I lived.

That same year, my manager, Charlane Cluett, had inadvertently sent a file to the wrong person. This set off a storm of anxiety in the agency about broken confidentiality. When the file was returned, my manager noticed that information in it hadn't been filed in the proper way. There should have had a cover sheet with the client's contact and other identifying information, third-party letters or notes, and client contact notes in a certain order. However, it was missing. Charlane called me in and asked me to do a file audit of all the active files of my eleven employees to see whether there were any more files like the errant one and to fix them. I was shocked. I was already over-extended doing the job of two area managers. I told her it would be impossible to do what she had asked. She asked how many I thought I could do. I said I could audit twenty-five percent of the files and she agreed.

As a result of the additional pressure, my blood pressure spiked and I had to see my family physician, Dr. Joan Lewis. She was a life saver. I'll never forget her caring consideration for my plight. She took the time to listen to me talk about my stressors and she authorized much needed and appreciated medical leave for me. This situation got me considering the option of finding work that had a more balanced pace. Self-care is talked about a lot among people in the caring professions. However, the profession attracts its fair share of workaholics and therapists driven to spend the better part of their energy helping others to the detriment of their own mental health. Indeed, I have come across therapists unsure they were performing up to standards they were unsure of. Witnessing these individuals and through my own experiences, I realized with even greater clarity the importance of taking a rest when we need it and being strong enough to acknowledge our own limitations and personal needs. As a result, I became more attuned to pacing myself and better at managing both my time and my commitments.

There was another factor that started our family thinking about making big changes. It seemed that the shadow was reappearing and especially pursuing my son. We would hear only after the fact about parties to which all his friends from school were invited. The straw that broke the camel's back was when Joy's colleague at the Huntsville hospital had a birthday party for his son, who was in the same class as our son. Many other boys from the class were invited, but not our son. Joy was especially miffed because she thought she enjoyed a good relationship with her colleague, who she would see and talk to at work occasionally. It seemed clear to us that he was being excluded because he was Black.

This led to a discussion between Joy and me about moving to ensure that our three children could experience their further development in a place where they would meet other Black children and experience acceptance and inclusion. We had enjoyed our time in Muskoka as a family mostly keeping to ourselves, with a weekly connection to our church family by going for walks with Eric and Eleanor Thorel and their son Jason on Saturdays after church, when the weather allowed. However, it was becoming increasingly evident that the integration of our children, especially our son, into the social life of the community was more of a challenge than we were willing to endure.

I began exploring employment options that would enable a move out of Muskoka. One involved discussion with Derrick Nichols, the president of the Ontario Conference of Seventh-day Adventists, and a return to being a pastor.

## A NEW CHAPTER IN OSHAWA

The negotiation was successful and soon we moved to Oshawa to begin a new chapter of our lives. I became the pastor of the Kendalwood Seventh-day Adventist Church, a racially mixed but mostly Black church, in Whitby, Ontario. The children were now away from Muskoka, where they had experienced the joys of rural living during short summers and long, snowbelt winters. They were away from being the only Black children in their classes. My eldest child, Hermione, was now studying to earn a degree in Communication with a minor in French at Andrews University in Berrien Springs, Michigan. My middle child, Hannah, was enrolled at Holy Trinity Catholic High School in Courtice, Ontario, and my son went to College Park Elementary School, a Seventh-day Adventist grade school in Oshawa. In a matter of months, Joy was able to secure a position as an assistant director of food services at Lakeridge Health, in their Oshawa hospital.

I began my return to being a pastor with a new perspective on my calling. When I was in England, my focus was on proving that I could function as a pastor who cared about his members, delivering weekly sermons consistent with the Adventist view of scripture and managing the operation of the Church faithfully. My years out of pastoral ministry, living briefly in the far north among the Indigenous people and then as a social worker working with the developmentally disabled and those with serious mental issues and crises, enabled me to approach my ministry from a different perspective.

I was no longer in the Adventist bubble every single week. I was seeing people who were struggling with their issues and I was grappling with ways of helping them that were practical and down to earth. I had helped people who were homeless locate options for housing in the community. I had helped people who were anxious with new ways of thinking about their fears. I had supported people with psychosis or developmental disabilities with accessing generic services in the community. Religious dogma did not necessarily help in those situations. Indeed, I found that religion sometimes gets in the way of common sense and practical solutions. So now, I was examining everything I believed. I wasn't swallowing the Adventist interpretation of scripture without thinking it through for myself. I would ask myself questions, such as whether a particular interpretation made sense. Were the traditional lifestyle practices of our church consistent with scripture, in my view?

With this renewed perspective, I decided I would continue being a pastor who cared for his members in a manner consistent with the ministry of Jesus. I would preach what I felt was biblical, meaning my focus would be on speaking about the grace of God, which sees everyone as a full member of the family of God–worthy of respect and worthy of eternal life. I would avoid berating members about their failures and focus on the goodness of God. I would avoid pointing out what Adventists believe are the errors of other denominations, which I find is a disturbing default position for many Adventists seeking to make themselves look good in the process.

I did exceptionally well at Kendalwood if you use the metrics of membership. When I came to the church, there were 350 members. By the time I left five years later, there were 450 members. Whether my ministry had the effect of making the church a more caring group of people, or whether members had more of a sense of being accepted by

God and more peaceful relationships with family, friends, neighbours, colleagues, and workmates, I'd leave that up to the assessment of members who experienced those benefits and to God.

I learned in my first years there that one of the White members had described me as a scallywag. I looked up the meaning in Google and found the following definition: "a term used in the old red-light district of Europe, referring to a scoundrel, troublemaker, or outlaw (or a troublemaker even among outlaws)."[18] There are other equally unflattering definitions. I wonder how that member came to that conclusion. Perhaps it was connected to a false rumour my head elder, Eric Buckley, shared with me that was making the rounds: that I was on my second marriage. It was clear to me, as is usually the case with such loose cannon statements, that the scallywag comment was more indicative of that person's state of mind than my own proclivities. In the five years, some (but not all) of the White members began to leave. Perhaps given my life experiences with the shadow companion, my racism antenna is hypersensitive. Ostensibly, the reasons always seemed innocent enough; they were mostly older members leaving to retire in rural areas.

One White member who didn't leave, Linda O'Connor, became my head elder. Her willingness to fill in for me at prayer meetings, her ability to preach, her faithful support of the program of the church by her attendance at many of its meetings, and the fact that she could share her opinions openly and make considered contributions to discussions on the church board made her an obvious choice. I also felt it important to

18. Fawkes, "Scallywag," Urban Dictionary, August 21, 2004, https://www.urbandictionary. com/define.php?term=skallywag.

have a person in leadership who reflected the tiny minority of White members because of my experience in the UK. It has stayed with me through all these years what it had felt like to be part of the Black British Seventh-day Adventist membership that at one point had felt isolated from decision-making in the church, having no Black pastors at the conference level.

Linda's support as my head elder was invaluable to me and helped me survive the last few months of my five years, from 2004 to 2009, as pastor at Kendalwood while I became increasingly convinced that I needed to transition away from pastoring again. I was increasingly at odds with the hardline views of members who were more oppositional in their relationships with people who didn't share our beliefs.

On one occasion, a group of boys was playing soccer in the church parking lot on a Saturday afternoon. We had no major meeting in the church at the time. There may have been a small group of people meeting, so there may have been a few cars in the parking lot (unlike on a Saturday morning, when church was in full swing for the major services of the week). Seeing these boys, one of the members told them angrily that it was our Sabbath and they couldn't play there. I had seen that same group of boys at a different time and, in a good-natured and friendly manner, asked what their names were and introduced myself to them.

At the next church board meeting, the member who had spoken angrily to the boys revealed what she had told them. I decided I needed to meet her attitude head on. I told the board members that it would have been a better approach if we could befriend the boys instead and invite them to use our parking lot whenever it was empty, which it pretty much was on every day of the week other than Saturday. Perhaps my use of what I felt was a teachable moment introduced a chill in the relationship I had with the church board and some other members of the church itself.

On another occasion, in 2009, we were going to host the visit of Admiral Barry Black, a distinguished Adventist who is currently the United States Senate Chaplain. We were going to need additional parking spaces other than what our church parking lot could provide. I went across the road to the local *masjid*, where Muslims met. The imam there said they would be happy to provide the additional parking spaces we needed.

Their willingness to accommodate us contrasted with the request many months earlier of the same imam, who had asked if our church could offer the young girls in their congregation classrooms during the week for their instruction, I'm guessing, in Arabic and in the Quran. I saw it as an excellent opportunity to build bridges with our Muslim neighbours. To my astonishment and great dismay, our church board was dead set against the request and some of the anti-Islamic comments made by one individual, a person of colour, were grossly shocking to me. I requested that a statement be included in the minutes expressing my opposition to the church board's decision and to some of the comments leading to denial of the imam's request for use of our classrooms, which were unused during each and every weekday.

I have tried to understand why a person of colour would harbour such anti-Islamic sentiments echoing the kind of vitriol usually voiced against Black people. Indeed, this autobiography focuses on the encounters I have had with the shadow of racial discrimination and prejudice. I have been on the receiving end of negative expectations of me before I even opened my mouth (as with a police officer I counselled who was sure I wouldn't do a good job when he first set eyes on me but confessed after our first session that he actually found me competent). So, I found it ironic that a Black church board member would fail to see how what he was articulating was the kind of prejudgment of a group of people that we have all felt. For him, the request from our Muslim neighbour conjured up the very worst images and ideas he had received about Muslims from the media, I'm guessing. He was doing the very same thing to taint the image in the minds of the other church board members that he himself would have been the target of by many in White society.

One doesn't need to be a trained mental health therapist like me to know what is at play here. Indeed, it is common knowledge that abused people can sometimes turn around and act as abusers. I remember, as a student back at Andrews University, talking with my Black friends about the beatings we had as children from our parents, who were doing the best they could to discipline us. We laughed ourselves silly as we described the beatings we received. It was interesting to me to learn, at the time, that my African-American friends had the same experiences of beatings. As descendants of slaves, we were recipients of the truth of the syndrome that people who have been subjected to unremittingly harsh treatment can be equally harsh to their offspring and to those around them, even generations later.

So as incomprehensible as it first appeared to me why that church board member would be so fuelled by his prejudice that he was adamant in denying the request of the Muslim congregation for access to our under-utilized classrooms, I understand on reflection the lasting harm that the shadow companion and the history of our shared past can do.

# STILL SERVING OTHERS, DESPITE THE SHADOW
## A CAREER CHANGE

By the end of 2009, I was ready to move on from pastoring. An opportunity to get back into counselling came up at Sir Sandford Fleming College in Peterborough, Ontario. I secured a part-time student counselling position that turned into a full-time position at the end of one year, after interviewing for a second time for the job I had been doing for just over a year previously. It irked me that I had to interview again for the exact same position I had been working at successfully and to the satisfaction of my supervisors, but I was told union rules dictated I go through this apparently redundant process.

I felt like I had now reached the pinnacle of my career. I was working as a counsellor, assisting students to overcome their obstacles and achieve academic success. I remembered absorbing with considerable pleasure the vibe at my alma mater, Andrews University, on a visit to explore it for my daughter Hermione a few years before and thinking I'd love to work in a post-secondary education setting. The atmosphere was vibrant, youthful, and energetic. And now here I was at Fleming College, working to help students of all ages but mostly young people. I was well-prepared with my experience as a pastor and more importantly, as a counsellor with experience in community mental health situations involving people with serious mental health issues. Although the problems were not always as severe in the college setting, I was equipped to offer interventions for issues related to mental health, relationships, academics, coping with daily living, and spirituality.

Over the ten years I was a counsellor at Fleming College, the issues became more severe, with anxiety and depression topping the list. It also became clear that lack of resilience was a growing problem among our younger students. The counselling department began to feel more like a community mental health agency. Before long, management took steps to limit the demands on our time due to the complexity of the issues with which we were dealing. At best, good faith efforts were being made to cope with the changing landscape of issues we were encountering. At worst, it felt at times that management was tinkering with our processes. Stricter limits were placed on the number of sessions we could offer students. Although professionally, we were supposed to be dispassionate and somewhat detached, it broke my heart when I had to inform a student that the limit on their sessions meant they were no longer eligible to receive counselling support at the college. There were tears and anger at the decision, which I didn't believe was in the best interest of the student–but orders were orders.

In addition, we were directed to refer students with more complex serious mental health issues to counsellors in the community. In my opinion, most students faced with this prospect found it an unwelcome barrier to service and declined those referrals.

I felt the tinkering had reached an unacceptable stage when a decision was taken to hive off disability, or so-called accessibility, services from psychotherapy services. This meant that if I was seeing a student for mental health problems and the student disclosed they had disability issues, I had to refer them to a colleague who specialized in those services. Students began to be bounced around to other counsellors in our department in addition to counsellors in the community.

A year before I left Fleming, our team of counsellors on the accessible education side and the psychotherapy side had a visit from the new president of the college. When she heard that the department had split the two services, she was bemused and asked why. Our director at the time stammered and had difficulty coming up with a cogent explanation. I felt for him because it really didn't make sense.

In my experience working in the community mental health setting, I had been exposed to provincial policy guidelines that extolled the virtues of so-called one-stop shopping, which attempted to cut down on the number of different professionals and agencies a client would have to encounter to receive effective service. In an effort to be in harmony with the policy, addiction services were co-located at the community mental health office where I was working as a counsellor in Huntsville. Prior to this move, if a counsellor referred a client to receive addiction services, they would have to travel to another location and, more often than not, the referral failed because the person just wouldn't show up at that other location. With the co-location of services, I could simply walk them to the addiction offices in the same building. Consequently, I understood the Fleming College president's confusion. Or at least, I think I did. Having students bounce around was not helpful. Having one counsellor offer both personal counselling and disability counselling made consummate sense.

Another issue I ran up against at Fleming was the intrusion, once again, of the shadow companion. Other than a colleague who had an Indigenous background and struggled with getting her voice heard, my other colleagues may never have been aware of it. I felt that suggestions I made in team meetings were met with indifference but when articulated by other White colleagues, they were lauded and adopted as worthy contributions. Eventually, I opted to take notes in meetings. This meant I didn't need to contribute to discussions as much, but simply focus on accurate recording of meetings.

A further manifestation of the same syndrome appeared to be at play when I volunteered to work on policies and procedures. The counselling department was operating without them when I got there. As a new employee when I was first hired, I had to rely exclusively on word-of-mouth instruction about my job and its expectations. I picked it up piecemeal as the months and years passed. Wherever I had worked previously, they had policy and procedure manuals I had to wade through to help familiarize myself with the expectations of my jobs. I was also experienced in drafting constitution and by-law documents in my work as a youth director for the SEC decades before. So when counsellors were asked to volunteer to work on projects not directly connected with counselling itself and one of those projects involved working on producing a policy and procedure manual, I jumped at the chance.

An interim manager had attempted to work on the same task some years earlier, but never really achieved much. Before we knew it, she was gone back to her old job in human resources at the college and that was the end of it. With whatever I could find from the little that the interim manager had accomplished, I, as the lead on the project, Audrey Healy, and one other counsellor, Laraine Hale, worked on drafting our policy and procedures.

It took about a year, with taking a few drafts to the larger group of counsellors to make sure we had their input along the way, before we had a policy and procedure manual to take to our director for approval and signature. An example of how such a document could be helpful was in reducing the frustration that took place whenever someone asked for vacation time off. This was a big pet peeve for me. The old way involved asking around if anyone else wanted the same time off and negotiating in a somewhat piecemeal fashion. There might be a meeting whenever the manager felt the time was right to finalize the vacation times, especially for the summer. It was frustrating because Joy and I really prized being able to take advantage of economical prices for winter vacations in January and February and waiting until March or April just didn't cut it for us. This method worked earlier on but as the department grew, it became unwieldy. The policy and procedure manual set out defined times for making vacation requests three times a year. The inspiration for this idea came from a procedure for requesting vacation times that my wife was familiar with in her position as a charge dietitian at Lakeridge Health.

I waited patiently at first for the policy and procedure manual to be approved and signed off by the director. As time went by and month after month passed, it became increasingly evident that he was dragging his feet for some reason. I will probably never know exactly why, but the spectre of the shadow companion did enter my imagination. Would he have dragged his feet if someone else had been the prime mover in making the project a reality? Was it just that he was inexperienced as a director and wanted more time to consider the policy and procedure document? Was it because he was irritated by me talking about the vacation policy and procedure–an irritation that was palpable whenever I brought it up? This was, after all, the same director who chose a counsellor with less seniority and experience than I had to be the counselling coordinator.

Again, I may never find out the reason behind his reluctance. But when a person who has been through what I have experienced from the shadows is faced with this kind of roadblock, I must wonder and seriously consider the possibility of the presence of my ubiquitous, ugly companion.

## A MOST PAINFUL EXPERIENCE

And now comes the most painful part of my story in recent times. I wrestled long and hard about whether I should include this part or whether I should lock it away and leave it in the vault of my memory and those of the one or two other people I told about it. However, I decided that this story wouldn't be complete without it. What I hope to achieve by bringing it out of the shadows is to alert younger family members to its blight, enabling them to be better equipped to see it and avoid its effects if possible.

I've had female students come to me with stories of reporting their ex-boyfriends or other males for various misdeeds. The stories made me extremely wary and careful about how I dealt with them. There was one student who activated my internal antennae, and I asked the administrative assistant to assign her to another counsellor so that there would never be any chance of accusations of impropriety. I had heard enough stories, especially involving teachers, of false accusations sprinkled among the genuine ones to make me hypervigilant. Those stories hardly ever appeared, in my mind, to end well. A teacher's career would be ruined by the accusation, their lives turned upside down. Their cases would be decided summarily by the judge and jury of the court of public opinion. In some cases, the accusing student would, trembling and penitent, confess that actually the story had been made up. Alas, it would be too late for the traumatized teacher.

When I worked in community mental health, a male colleague had been the target of such an accusation. I witnessed how traumatic it was for him. He was devastated and walked around under a cloud for weeks. I remember how in our team meetings, he used to give excellent, incisive reports of cases he was dealing with. As a counsellor new to my craft, I was in awe of him. I don't know if he ever recovered from that situation and he subsequently left the agency to work elsewhere. I was determined it would never happen to me, hence my hypervigilance.

In 2019, during my tenth year of working at Fleming College, a student came to see me. The first thing I noticed was that she had an extremely low-cut top on. Her rather ample bosom could be clearly seen without any effort. When it emerged that she had more severe underlying mental health issues, I suddenly welcomed the new protocol of referring her to an external counselling agency for ongoing psychotherapy and was happy to quickly take steps to do so.

My only task was to bridge her to that help, which involved someone else in the department assigned to assist with this. I also worked to bridge her to disability accommodations, which took a further couple of sessions. Given her attire at the first session, I instinctively thought moving her along was a definite plan that I reasoned would minimize any risk of false accusations.

Imagine my utter surprise when I discovered she had accused me of sexual impropriety. I was devastated. Despite my best efforts, here I was facing the very thing I feared. That fear had motivated me to pay, year after year for decades, for professional liability insurance even when fellow colleagues were declining to pay for it. I had a sense that if I was accused of any impropriety, my employers would throw me under the bus. That, I reasoned, was the nature of an organization: protecting the organization first and foremost appears to be the mantra guiding most, if not all, of them–Fleming College included.

I now knew how my colleague must have felt years before, and there were lots more surprises to come. One was that the very counsellor in the community who the student had been referred to, facilitated by me, was instrumental in helping her make the complaint. I had to decide whether to fight it. Doing so took a tremendous toll on my own mental health but at first, there was the instinctive impulse to clear my name. I am a retired ordained minister. I reasoned that accusations leaking out, even though devoid of any confirming evidence, would hurt my reputation. My church organization would hear about it and I doubted whether the lofty standard of "innocent until proven guilty" would be applied.

The college engaged a lawyer to conduct an investigation. I had the support of my union representative. Apart from the union rep, my sole support was my wife Joy who stood by me through it all. As time went on and like a snowball rolling downhill, the accusation appeared to blossom and take on proportions way beyond a "he said, she said" scenario, so I engaged a lawyer of my own through my professional liability insurance. My decision to pay for liability insurance early in my counselling career was vindicated.

The advice I received from my lawyer didn't leave me with a whole lot of confidence about my chances of successfully clearing my name. It was my word against the student's. My lawyer advised me that the investigation could very well escalate. She also said the Ontario College of Social Workers and Social Service Workers could get involved and they would launch their own investigation. Information about the incident could become public and as far as I could see, I would be fair game for the speculation of people who would have zero context before passing judgment, positive or negative. I had witnessed that very thing happening to people in the media and frankly, I wanted to avoid it like the proverbial plague.

At first, I was confident there was absolutely no evidence that could be used against me. The student reported her version of what happened in my office scribbled on scraps of paper. No one else was present. But as time went by, the lawyer for the college started to bring in additional unrelated accusations from other departments at the college, one of which was characterized as unwelcomed friendliness on my part toward women in the Financial Aid Office (FAO). It felt like the college's lawyer was functioning like a North Sea trawler that I had learned about when I was a kid in school. The trawler would drag a net behind it, scooping up fish of all shapes and sizes and then hoisting it up out of the water onto its deck with its catch dripping and wriggling as they made their last efforts to get oxygen. The lawyer was hoisting reports from various quarters casting me in a negative light.

This was unnerving to me, especially since I had prized myself on establishing a good working relationship with the FAO to achieve the best help possible for my students. Sometimes a student needed something from the FAO to enable them to grease their financial wheels, whether it was help with approving bursaries or expediting financial aid from the Province of Ontario. At times, I could achieve better success for the student if I went and presented their case personally instead of leaving it to the student, who may not be aware of how best to present their situation. I knew who best to go to in the FAO; I knew who specialized in whichever aspect of their request. So, I was shocked when this working relationship I had established to successfully help my students was now being used as evidence of impropriety. In addition, it was presented as evidence of a pattern that, despite no concrete evidence of anything untoward between me and the student, could be used to establish that something bad must have happened on balance. The term "witch hunt" seems appropriate to describe what the college's lawyer was doing.

For me, that was the kicker. I thought about fighting the student's accusations. I thought about my age as, at almost 70, I should have already retired. I thought about the toll it was taking on me mentally and physically. I reasoned that claims and counterclaims would take on a life of their own and spiral into the months and years of investigations that my lawyer told me were a possibility, drawing in my professional college and even my church. I didn't think I could handle what I predicted would be sustained psychological pressure. I didn't think I could get used to month after month, and in all likelihood year after year, enduring sleepless nights, constantly ruminating about what happened and what I could have done differently to protect myself. I remember going to meet the college's lawyer to hear evidence against me–how Joy was made to wait outside and how I would get a terrible itch on the sole of my foot, an obvious nervous reaction. I could hardly think straight as the itch would begin and the lawyer started to ask me questions.

Another unnerving realization came when the lawyer would put one of the student's accusations to me that she had scribbled in barely legible handwriting. The lawyer asked if I remembered what she said happened. I told him I saw over a hundred students in a semester and I did not recall such a thing happening. The lawyer noted that the student remembered it clearly and used this against me. I was staggered that he was able to come to that conclusion. How was I to know that stating I was unable to recall an incident is often interpreted as a guilty person deflecting their culpability? I wondered afterwards whether I would have fared differently if I had lied and claimed perfect recall of the accused behaviour not happening.

I decided I wouldn't fight it. I reasoned that even if I was successful, I might have to wade through accusations from other departments, other staff members, and perhaps even other colleagues with their negative slant on my actions, though innocent, like the ones the staff in the FAO had supplied. I made my decision even though the lawyer for the college eventually found no evidence of sexual impropriety and downgraded the situation to a finding of harassment. Fortunately, a retirement package was offered to Fleming faculty and I jumped at the chance to get out and leave it all behind. I'm an ordained minister but unlike many other of my fellow church members, I don't see the hand of God in every tiny detail of my life at the best of times. Yet with the fortuitous announcement of the retirement package, I felt like God was looking out for me and had given me a dignified way out of the mess.

At least I thought I had left it all behind. A few months after I officially retired, I received a letter from Fleming College informing me they decided they had a duty to report the whole incident to my professional college. The effect was that I eventually decided to resign my membership all because of a student's unsubstantiated accusations.

It left a nasty taste in my mouth. If I could go back and relive it all, I would have video recording in my office as the camera would have substantiated my position. But even that may not have helped. What about the aspersions cast on my behaviour by other staff—one, at least, who was never named? Unfolding around the time of the whole Black Lives Matter situation, I doubted I could rely on a fair process. I had seen reports in the media about racially motivated violence against Black people. I read about racial inequality experienced by Black people who encountered the legal system, including the police and the courts both in the United States and in Canada. I heard from the international students, especially those from India I'd counselled, that they felt an atmosphere of racism existing at Fleming College and I felt that perhaps there was more to their sensibilities than met the eye. I didn't feel like taking my chances at receiving a favourable outcome if I contested it, especially against that backdrop. The shadow companion appeared to be present once more, but in a more menacing, life-changing way than ever before.

To this day, when I wake up at night or at odd times during the day, I find my mind sometimes meandering to that whole situation. A jumble of thoughts penetrates my consciousness. Why did it happen? What did the student get out of reporting the claims? Was the student hyper-anx-

The author in his late sixties
taken 2022

ious, perhaps due to substance abuse? I sometimes fantasize about how one day, the student will confess that nothing untoward happened in my office. Then after toying for a fleeting moment with the satisfaction of that happening, my rational mind takes over and the scenario recedes like steam evaporating into the background. The student would have to find Jesus or Buddha, I think, for that to happen. Yet although extremely unlikely, there's a sliver of a chance of it happening, which means I'll probably toy with that slim-to-none eventuality until my last breath.

## WORKING AMONG ABORIGINAL PEOPLE

Now, I found myself in a state of forced retirement. I had started to plan for retirement a couple of years earlier. During my working life, I always said that I'd keep working into my sixties, seventies, and beyond. I liked my work and besides, because I'd had breaks in my work life where I didn't pay into a pension, I felt that continuing to do the work I loved as a counsellor would give me income security. My plan involved being registered as a social worker with the Manitoba College of Social Workers so I could work as a mental health therapist in Aboriginal communities in northern Manitoba. I had heard about the opportunity from my friend, Peggy Anderson, who is a Nurse in Charge in one of those Aboriginal communities.

By the time circumstances forced me to retire, I was well along in my application to the Manitoba College of Social Workers. I just had a few more documents to provide, including evidence of awareness of First Nations issues. My year in Moose Factory, when Joy was working as a Diabetes Coordinator for the Mushkegowuk Council, formed a part of my evidence. So was my attendance at cultural awareness events at Fleming College and the endorsement of Kylie Fox, who was working with Aboriginal students at Fleming College and promoting their interests. I also had counselled Aboriginal clients in my short time in private practice.

I was now ready to apply to Health Canada's First Nations Inuit Health Branch (FNIHB) to find work in Northern Manitoba. My application was successful and the first request I saw from them was to work in the Aboriginal community of God's Lake Narrows (GLN). My work there would consist of being available for round-the-clock crisis intervention. One reason why I and three other mental health therapists were called to work up in GLN was because there had been a spate of suicides over the previous few years. The situation culminated in August 2019 with the suicide of a young teenager. Her suicide sparked a few more teenage suicides, which triggered a state of emergency called for by the chief of the Keewatin Band Council. A couple of months into my time there, one of my colleagues showed me a picture on her cellphone of three teenage girls she had been working with in 2019. All three were now deceased, lives tragically claimed by suicide.

My start in GLN began with a flight from Toronto's Pearson International Airport to Winnipeg. I stayed in a hotel overnight and the following morning, I took a Perimeter Aviation plane from Winnipeg to GLN. GLN is a community located 550 kilometres northeast of Winnipeg. The best way to get there is flying one and a half hours or, in the winter, driving approximately 20 hours using the winter roads, some of which cross frozen lakes. If you have ever watched the reality television show *Ice Road Truckers*, GLN was featured in Season 7 of the show. The population is almost all Indigenous. The area has been a favourite of American tourists who come up north to fish. Locals act as their guides on the water.

On my first trip up north while I waited in the Perimeter Aviation lounge, a humble room accommodating both departures and arrivals, I saw a young Aboriginal lady looking somewhat worse for wear in terms of both her attire and physical appearance. She was pacing up and down, speaking loudly and generally drawing attention to herself. I tried to ignore the disturbance she was creating. To my surprise, she singled me out, accusing me of staring at her and making her feel uncomfortable. With the recent trauma of a false accusation at Fleming College in mind, I was immediately thrown into trauma mode. I remember thinking to myself, "Here we go again, and I haven't even started in the community." What an introduction to my work there!

My first rotation would be for six days in September, the second for ten days, and pretty soon I would have a regular rotation each month of ten days. This would subsequently be reduced to eight days a month, much to my considerable relief.

A few days after I arrived for my very first rotation and started to see clients in community, I had a referral to see a young lady. To my horror, it was the same young lady I had encountered in the Perimeter Aviation lounge. I was shocked. My instinct was to tell the receptionist that I didn't want to see her for mental health therapy. I thought I would be at high risk for further accusations. Despite this, I did see her and wondered at first if she remembered the incident. It turned out later in subsequent sessions that she did indeed remember, but perhaps was behaving erratically under the influence of a substance at the time. It gives me great satisfaction to know that I was able to work past my initial post-traumatic fears and apprehensions and to do all that I could to help her to cope with and improve her circumstances.

Working for FNIHB in GLN was an eye-opener on the way the Government of Canada deals with Aboriginal communities. I worked in the nursing station there. I liked the set-up because the accommodation and clinic for the nurses, doctor, and mental health therapists were all under one roof. A few other nursing stations were separated from the living quarters I heard, which was challenging in the heart of the frigid winters in the north.

As I reflected on the cause of the 12 suicides that had prompted the call for additional mental health therapists and what to do about the situation, I remember noting that facilities for the youth were limited. I heard about a place, I'm not sure whether it was a hall or a room, that had some weightlifting equipment, but it was closed the whole time (just over a year) that I worked in the community. There was no high school in GLN. Children had to leave the community and go to Winnipeg or another larger city than the Narrows to receive a high school education. Many lost their way in those places, disconnected from family and their home community. A high school was being built while I worked in GLN, promising relief from that less-than-ideal situation. Still, addictions were a huge issue in the community.

The local people were bewildered by the way crystal meth use had crept into the community and, in a few short years, devastated it. The user often experienced changes in personality and disruptions in their relationships. Often it led to lack of ambition or drive to be productive and work. Efforts to meet the issue of addiction with legal enforcement were stymied, from what I heard, by threats to the lives and safety of well-meaning individuals tasked with that responsibility from within the community.

I came to the conclusion that there were no easy answers to the challenges faced in GLN and many other Aboriginal communities like it in Manitoba and other Canadian provinces. I had to confess to myself that I honestly couldn't see a solution to their issues. I did come up with a few observations I thought might be helpful as a starting point. I wrote the following in response to a request from the GLN Council in its own search for solutions:

### Recommendations to Address the Suicidal Ideations, Attempts, and Problems with the Youth

1. It goes without saying that the root causes need to be addressed, e.g. availability of drugs, and parenting issues.
2. Strong efforts must be made to completely eliminate the importing of crystal meth into the community, as a matter of urgent priority. This may involve dangerous undercover policing since vested interests will no doubt seek to preserve the trade.
3. Have sniffer dogs at the airport to monitor for drugs.
4. Family preservation workers need to be hired for "in-home" teaching of parenting skills, in addition to providing public education about

parenting via the local radio station and national media outlets.

5. Youth recreational facilities need to be improved/provided and full-time youth workers hired to run daily programs, monitor use of sports and workout/gym equipment. A budget needs to be available for depreciation and ongoing replacement of equipment (e.g., hockey equipment, basketballs, nets, weights, workout/multi-gym machines, etc.).

6. Encourage a public education program where local youth can share success stories of overcoming or resisting drug use.

7. Improve the availability of workers to offer outdoor/camping/hunting/trapping/fishing education for youth.

Of course, much of what lay at the heart of the issues experienced by Aboriginal communities is rooted in the colonial past and its current legacies. I read about the experience of Jody Wilson-Raybould, former Minister of Justice and Attorney General of Canada, the first Indigenous person to hold the office. CBC News announced in a post on July 8, 2021, that she had decided not to run for re-election, pointing to a "toxic" environment in Parliament and a "focus on partisanship rather than achieving positive change for Canadians." Included in the Canadians she referred to were Aboriginal Canadians and the lip service paid to improving their circumstances.

Looking back on my experience in Aboriginal communities, that is, living in Moose Factory, Ontario, for a year and working in GLN, I wondered why, despite the wealth of natural, manufacturing, and financial resources Canada boasts, I had witnessed substandard housing, including poor insulation, in those communities. Why was I hearing from my clients about lack of housing and multi-generational families living in cramped conditions? Why was it I was hearing about problems with clean drinking water in some Aboriginal communities?

I also recall a talk given in GLN by an Aboriginal man based in the United States, who talked about Aboriginal communities and pre-colonial contact and their proud heritage of stable families with none of the issues of substance abuse.

I could only conclude that there is a lack of will to seriously address some of the current issues in those communities—one that is too easy to blame on the communities themselves. It is a lack that is obviously rooted in colonial attitudes honed and shaped in an era that needed to justify the White European subjugation of Indigenous people and their land. The murky shadow of these attitudes hangs menacingly, like a dark autumn cloud, over contemporary Canadian society.

A patent example of those colonial attitudes emerges from the interpretation the Seventh-day Adventist Church has of a pet prophecy found in the Bible in Revelation 13. In this prophecy, two beasts are depicted. One is a sea beast. The sea, according to Adventist prophetic decoding, refers to a place teeming with people. That beast is seen as emerging from the teeming millions in Europe. The other beast is an earth beast. The earth is decoded by Adventists as a place that is uninhabited or sparsely populated. That beast is seen as a power, namely the United States, emerging in North America during the eighteenth and nineteenth centuries. One can only conclude that the millions of Aboriginal people who existed in North America from sea to shining sea were regarded as insignificant or, as my African-American friends would say, "no-count." This is the same syndrome leading people to promote the idea that Christopher Columbus "discovered" people in the Caribbean.

This view of the United States of America emerging in an unpopulated area of the world is manifestly dark, carrying with it the shadow of racist attitudes and the idea that the lives the Europeans encountered did not matter. It is a matter of record that those attitudes, which were fashioned and propagated to justify slavery, were the same attitudes that justified the genocide and land grab that ensued.

Sadly, it is a prophetic understanding that has not been addressed and challenged at the highest levels of the Church. It basically has not been spotted on the radar of Church hierarchy as an issue deserving of attention. A few years ago at an evangelistic campaign, a series of meetings designed to try to attract more members into the Church, a pastor of the College Park Seventh-day Adventist Church pontificated about Revelation 13. I attended that presentation to see if his preparation and theological scholarship had led him to adjust the interpretation of the prophecy and update it in the light of modern anti-racist sentiments. To my dismay, he repeated the old lines of the interpretation: the United States had emerged on a continent that was desolate and unpopulated! My father, with his distinct brand of humour, would have said my "gasted was well flabbered." I was indeed flabbergasted and disappointed. Racist attitudes were alive and well in the Church and its presentation of the interpretation of Biblical prophecy.

The effect this has had on my mind and on the minds of other theologians, especially but not exclusively those of colour, is to call into question Adventist interpretations of prophecy that have been thrown into sharp relief as Eurocentric, perpetuating the sidelining of darker hued peoples of the world. In spite of this, I have remained a member of the Church even while deeply disturbed by some of its official beliefs. Perhaps I am a living embodiment of a syndrome I witness in my reading of slavery, wherein many slaves became Christians (the religion of the slave masters). It could be argued that the slaves carried with them from Africa, and passed on to their children born into slavery, a belief in God that allowed them to see the inconsistencies in the religion of the slave masters. It possibly allowed them to sift out the inhumane brutality meted out to them and to see in the Bible the God of liberation and freedom they always knew. Perhaps they found resilience and a sense of hope in the belief that, in the words of Martin Luther King, Jr., the "moral arc of the universe bends towards justice."

So, here I am, also seeing inconsistencies in my own church and its understanding of scripture but seeing past them and between the lines of a Bible that introduces themes of equity, justice, and fairness even as it also exposes on its pages the foibles and failings of human beings writ large. My father modelled that approach to life and believed in the message of the Bible and the Seventh-day Adventist Church, with all its faults, until his dying day. His example has been a guiding light for me, although I am a great deal more critical of the Church than he ever was. I have found my niche in church life helping those needing food at the New Life Neighbourhood Centre located at and run by my church.

For me, the emphasis of my spiritual experience is on helping others rather than on being correct in doctrinal interpretation and claiming that my denomination is the one true Church (a ridiculous proposition in my view and of others in my church).

## PROCESSING MY EXPERIENCES

This brings me up to the present day. Retired now, I am trying to live my senior years with less drama and shelter as much as I can from the gloomy interactions of the shadowy kind that I've been describing in this book. The reality is that one cannot escape this persistent companion who interjects itself into every aspect of life. During the pandemic, there were reports of communities of Black, Indigenous, and People of Colour (BIPOC) being exponentially more exposed to the harsh economic devastations caused by COVID-19. They tended to have more of the jobs that involved frontline contact with people. They didn't have jobs that extended paid sick leave or would transition to work from home.

If I was still working as a counsellor at Fleming College or if I had continued private practice counselling, I could have transitioned to telephone counselling and kept working without interruption. I had generous sick time allowances, which meant I could be paid while off sick with COVID if I contracted it. Those mostly BIPOC frontline workers who were serving coffee, cleaning hospital rooms, caring for the sick, and working in grocery stores didn't have the luxury of transitioning so easily, nor were they compensated in a way that allowed them to continue to earn money without interruption as I would have been. It frustrated me immensely to see the harshness of the way society is divided, with those doing the hardest of jobs being rewarded less. The COVID-19 crisis brought this out into sharp relief.

In recent times, the mass graves of Indigenous children in Canada have come to light. The complicity of the Christian Church, both Catholic and Protestant, in this heinous situation brought to the fore their scant regard for BIPOC lives. During the pandemic, I had more time to reflect on these characterizations, including the complicity of the Christian Church in slavery. I also had time to read books such as *The Warmth of Other Suns* by Isabel Wilkerson, which charted the migration of Black Americans from the south to the north to escape White southern terrorism. I also read another of Isabel Wilkerson's books, *Caste*, about an artificial hierarchy that exists globally but sees its most perverted form in North America, with Black people at the bottom of that hierarchy.

Consequently, I have less hope in solutions to the deleterious effects of the legacy of slavery. I am not confident of change in the future, given the propaganda Christian Europe and its North American sons and daughters contrived to make it palatable to regard non-White people as 'less-than' in the process of becoming the behemoth and wealthy "First World" built since the sixteenth century.

I can't see this situation ever changing. I used to try to talk myself into a hopeful attitude. As an ordained minister of religion, speaking about and believing in a hope despite appearances to the contrary is evidence that one is a good Christian. But I find this kind of hope elusive today. My forefathers in bondage kept going and perhaps they managed to do so because they had the kind of faith in God and a better future, a faith that the Bible defines as the "substance of things hoped for, the evidence of things not seen." I am aware of the God-fearing African forefathers who, before European chattel slavery, built thriving societies in the cradle of human civilization and served a God who in Scripture promises a radical transformation of the world. But with every emerging historical fact about Europe's past and with every realization of its current legacies that have enabled the institution of colonialism and chattel slavery to morph into economic imperialism, it becomes increasingly difficult for me to see an escape from its dark enduring reality.

It wasn't until the present time that I developed a clearer view of what my cousin Dr. Jerome Crichton explains as the problem: that Whites in general have been brought up, or socialized, to believe in their supe-riority and are blithely unaware of the privileged position they occupy in society.

In addition, in later years I have come to understand the whole concept of *White Fragility*, the title of a book by Robin DiAngelo. In the book, she expertly describes the pathological sensitivity of Whites in relation to the truth of how White people have related to Black people for centuries, up to and including the present day. Indeed, the news of the day at the time of writing is the vote-grabbing quest of Ron DeSantis, Governor of Florida, pandering to the pathological need of his White supporters to suppress in his state any truth about the vagaries of White supremacy. He is leading them in a crusade, with all the historical nega-tivity that the word "crusade" implies, against so-called critical race theory, a patently clear outgrowth of this pathological sensitivity. Its most senseless and idiotic example is the banning by Governor DeSantis of elementary school mathematics books that he and his ilk purport to contain what they consider to be critical race theory.

The only hope I am left with is that while contemporary institutions and societies may function to breathe life into the shadow companion, the associations I have with people on an individual level–whatever their background–can be meaningful and mutually respectful. In my work as a counsellor and as a pastor, I have met individuals who engaged me in a mutually respectful way. Some were willing to understand the Black experience and learn from it how to relate as human to human. To my White friends, I say work past the guilt of the terrible practices of your forefathers and open yourselves up to learning from us, the descendants of slaves, how to be resilient in the face of inhumane odds. To my Black friends, I say work past the indoctrination that places you at a starting point of slavery and reach back to see the legacy of your glorious African ancestors and recover the stolen stories of your heritage. To my Black friends, I also say look at what we've achieved in spite of the blight of colonialism. We are among the ultimate survivors.

All of us are caught up in the enduring legacy of the past. My only comfort is in following Jesus' challenge to adhere to the Golden Rule and do unto others what I would have them do unto me, to love others as I love myself, and to seek out and associate with people of like mind. This way of living has been my guiding principle. Even though I've been hurt in life, relating to others with graciousness, kindness, and equity has enabled me to experience deep satisfaction and joy in the midst of it all. So, this is not a tale of unmitigated woe.

Being on the receiving end of kindness, including the graciousness of White people such as the doctor, a complete stranger who lent me his car for a weekend, or Mrs. Giraud, the landlady who rented to my parents in their early days as new immigrants in England in the 1950s, impressed on me that no one group of people has a monopoly on goodness and fairness. I also think about the police officer I counselled, who initially had doubts about my competence or ability to help him but was able to see past his prejudice and embrace my help. I recall the Appalachian people in Ohio who received my chaplain support with open-heartedness when they came to the hospital to grieve the death of their loved ones. Indeed, it has helped me to pay their kindness forward, giving people the benefit of the doubt in my interactions with them regardless of their ethnic background. It has bolstered my own resilience knowing that I am not alone on life's journey and can rely on support from fair-minded people regardless of their ethnicities.

This is where I find my hope. I find it one individual at a time, one person who works past the prejudice they've been socialized to practice and instead acts with mutual respect. Perhaps this will ultimately chip away at the blight of racism and gradually dispel the darkness of the Shadow Companion with the light of their kindness and willingness to relate with equity and fairness.

And Almighty God will have to take care of the rest.